COCK

BEHAVIOUR

Understanding your Cockapoo's Behaviour and Learning to Deal with Problems Effectively

WRITTEN BY

DR. GORDON ROBERTS BVSC MRCVS

Hello! My name is Gordon Roberts and I'm the author of this book. I hope you enjoy all of the specialist advice it contains. I'm a huge advocate of preventative care for animals, and I'd love to see more pet owners taking the time to research their pet's health care needs.

Being proactive and educating yourself about your pet's health now, rather than later on, could save you and your pet a lot of trouble in the long run.

If you'd like to read more of my professional pet care advice simply go to my website at http://drgordonroberts.com/freereportsdownload/.

As a thank you for purchasing this book, you'll find dozens of bonus pet care reports there to download and keep, absolutely free of charge!

Best wishes,

Gordon

Founder, Wellpets

Introduction:
The no. 1 way to avoid Cockapoo behavioural issues

As you take the time to learn all about the behaviour of the Cockapoo, there is one important thing you should know. The number one way to avoid getting a Cockapoo with behavioural issues is simply to get your Cocka from a reputable breeder. Whilst many bad behaviours can be nipped in the bud, if you can avoid them altogether you should. And the best way to do that is to get a dog that has been raised in a good environment, with well-behaved dogs in its bloodline.

If your Cocka pup is brought up in an unstable or isolated environment, for example, if they have very little contact with humans or if they aren't used to other animals, there is a good chance that they will have behavioural problems. They might be fearful and even develop aggression later on in life. It's also really important to know the temperament of the mother, since puppies can often inherit these traits from their parents. A good breeder will know all about these issues and will more than likely have taken measures to avoid them.

Where can I find a good breeder?

There are lots of ways to find a breeder these days. You could try:
- An internet search for breeders in your area
- Visiting dog shows and speaking to breeders face to face
- Asking dog owners you know where they found their breeders
- The UK Kennel Club is an organisation dealing with canine health, training and welfare. Their website has a directory of approved breeders who have met their quality standards.

What makes a good breeder

Once you've found a breeder that you like the sound of, it's time to visit them and their dogs to check how reputable they are. A good breeder:
- Doesn't breed dogs to order and will usually only breed about 2 or 3 litters a year
- Is a real dog lover and has plenty of useful information to share about their breed
- Lets you visit the puppies while they're still with their mother
- Keeps the puppies in the family home
- Takes a real interest in the health and temperament of all their dogs
- Really cares about their puppies going to a good home
- Takes the time to socialise the puppies before they leave their care, getting them used to contact with other people and animals

What questions should you ask the breeder?

When you go to visit the puppies, it's important to take a good look around to make sure they're well cared for. Inspect the puppies and their mothers for signs of illness. Here are some useful questions to ask while you're there:

- How old are the puppies?
- Are they fully weaned (off their mother's milk)?
- Can I see the puppies with their mother?
- How old is the mother, and does she have a good temperament?
- How many litters has the mum had?
- Are the puppies wormed and vaccinated?
- When is the next dose of vaccination due?
- What diet is the puppy on, and can I take some with me so I can gradually wean him off it?

What to avoid

Not all puppies are bought directly from a breeder. Some are bought in pet shops and puppy farms, both of which are a really bad idea. Puppies from these places can be very unhealthy and it's important not to support any trade which doesn't put animal welfare first.

Rescued Cockas

Rescue shelters often get puppies, and it can be very rewarding to give them a good home. The good thing is that most shelters will have given each puppy a full veterinary examination. The puppy will usually be fully wormed, vaccinated and micro-chipped.

They will have also had an assessment to make sure they have the right temperament to be re-homed, which is great news for prospective dog owners. You'll probably need to have a home visit from a member of shelter staff to be sure that you're a suitable owner and your house has enough space to keep a dog.

It's important to note that you might have to work a little harder with a rescue puppy to win its trust and affection, especially if the pup has been mistreated. You'll probably know less about the puppy's background and health history, and they might need a bit more training and socialisation than other dogs. It's worth it to see a pup find its "forever home".

Why you should choose carefully

This is a decision that should be made with care - after all, you're going to be spending the next 10-14 years with your dog. The last thing you want is to come home with a pup that's too timid (leading to behavioural issues) or too pushy (making him difficult to train). In addition, there is a risk that you will take home a very innocent looking pup who may turn out to have health issues. This is one of the reasons that you should resist the urge to go for the tiniest, quietest pup in the litter – there may well be a reason this pup is cowering in the corner.

Temperament tests for Cockapoo pups

The Cockapoo is famed for his wonderful, friendly temperament and eagerness to please. He should be gentle natured without being timid, and confident without being too domineering, so be as observant as you can when you go to view the litter. Here are some useful tests you can do.

Test 1: Observation
Sit and watch the puppies for a few minutes. Which ones are playing happily with each other, and which ones are shying away from their siblings? Ideally you want a sociable puppy that is happy playing with the others in the litter. Look for one that is neither too submissive nor too dominant with the other pups - somewhere in the middle is a good choice.

Test 2: Handling
Pick up the Cockapoo you like the best and see how he reacts to being handled. Cradle the pup on his back and see what he does. If he reacts badly, and seems very upset, you should choose a different pup. A puppy with a good temperament will wriggle and show some resistance at first, but will then settle down and accept being cuddled.

Test 3: Play time
See how the puppy responds to being played with. Does he show a keen interest in playing with you? Or does he simply look away?

Choose a pup that seems playful with plenty of energy and a zest for life.

Test 4: Loud noises

Take a set of keys out and shake them above your pup's face. Does he look up quickly, show surprise and then look away. Or does he cower away? Maybe he reacts aggressively? The first of these is a sign of a good temperament – a puppy that looks startled at first and then loses interest.

Meeting the mother

Apart from meeting all the puppies, don't forget to spend some time with their mother. This will give you a good indication of what the temperament of the pups will be once they are fully grown. She should be gentle, friendly, happy and relaxed. She should also be well trained and used to strangers. If you can tick all of these boxes, you have probably chosen wisely. Good luck!

Understanding how the Cockapoo's history affects its behaviour

Let's learn about where this special little dog came from and how he became a popular breed in his own right. Firstly, remember that your Cockapoo is a mixture of the Cocker Spaniel and the Poodle. Knowing the history of both of these breeds is going to be important when it comes to understanding your dog and what makes him tick. And of course, your Cockapoo might show more of one breed's behaviour than the other, depending on whether he comes from parents with more Poodle blood or more Cocker blood.

The Cocker Spaniel's history

Back in Roman times, a variety of dog types were bred to fulfil every-day tasks such as guarding property, hauling and hunting. From these dogs there emerged some distinct groups, including:
Guarding dogs
Shepherd dogs
Sporting dogs
War dogs
Scent dogs
Sight dogs

Many of these are the founding breeds of today's modern dog types and most dogs can be traced back to one of the above categories. As you can guess, the Cocker Spaniel is probably descended from the scent dogs, or hounds as they were later known.

Hounds were developed to chase and hunt down prey until it was either cornered or exhausted, wherein it would be killed. However, hunters soon realised that these dogs could chase prey for miles, which wasn't very productive for the purposes of catching food. Instead, some clever hunters began to breed dogs that would simply track down the scent of game and flush it out from the undergrowth, or wherever it happened to be hiding.

This was before the days of guns, so sometimes these hunters trained hawks to catch wildfowl that had been flushed out by their dogs. These scent hounds were very obedient and were a little bit more composed, waiting patiently for their master's commands. They had to have good temperaments and the ability to get on well with other dogs, because they were often brought out to hunt in groups.

By the Middle Ages, many of these dogs used for flushing out wild-fowl originated from Spain. It's thought that the word Spaniel came from the Latin word for Spain, which is Hispania, which later became "Spaniels".

From these early Spaniels came the English, Irish and Gordon Setters who were trained to drop close to the ground and remain there stock still until their masters came to trap their quarry with nets. As for the remaining Spaniels, they were trained to sniff out prey and they were bred to have a medium size and powerful legs so that they could easily push their compact bodies through the undergrowth in search of game. Their long wavy coats protected their skin from brambles which fell from the fur easily rather than becoming lodged there. To stop their tails catching in the brush, their owners began the practice of docking their tails.

These Spaniels became known for their happy-go-lucky temperaments and their tendency to follow their masters everywhere. Some Spaniels became experts at tracking woodcock, and they were known as Cocking Spaniels. In the late 19th century, breeders set about separating the Spaniel breeds into different categories. The Cocking Spaniels became the Cocker Spaniels and they fell into this category if they weighed under 28lb. Those that were more than 28lb were the Field Spaniels, and separate again from these were the Water Spaniels.

The Cocker Spaniel was registered with the American Kennel Club in 1879. Much later, in 1946, breeders in America successfully established a further division within the Cocker Spaniel breed – there became a recognised English Cocker Spaniel as well as a separate, distinct American Cocker Spaniel. The American Cocker had longer legs and a shorter back than the English Cocker and there were far more of them in the U.S. Today, both breeds are extremely popular throughout the world.

The Poodle's history

The Poodle is a very old breed of dog and pictures of its ancestors can be found in Ancient Egypt and on Roman artefacts as early as 30AD. In these pictures they are shown bringing in nets and collecting catches from the marshes. So, we know that this breed was originally bred to be happy in water. The word Poodle actually came from an ancient German word (pudeln) that means "to splash in water". They can also be seen in late 14th century artworks and writings

(Conrad Gesner in 1353) pulling milk carts and hunting for truffles, but it wasn't until the late 1800s that the Poodle Club listed the first breed standard. It's thought that they originated in Germany and came to France with German soldiers.

The three sizes of Poodle have been around for hundreds of years. The toy versions in particular became known as "sleeve dogs" along with other small breeds of dog, simply because they could be used as hot water bottles for the hands and were kept in the sleeves of the nobility during the Renaissance (14-17th centuries). In France, the Poodle became popular in the circus and in the Royal Courts of Europe where they became popular as pets.

The distinct clipping of Poodles stems way back to when they were working dogs and because they were in the water a lot of the time, the thick fur around their hind legs slowed them down in the water and made them tire more easily, so was shaved away. To keep their vital organs warm while in water the fur around these areas was left in its natural state. It is thought that the topknot was tied with a thread to distinguish it from other Poodles while working.

It wasn't until the end of the 19th century that the Poodle started to become popular in the UK, then after World War II they reached a peak in popularity. In the 1960s they were the most popular breed in the US and was the breed that was registered the most with the American Kennel Club.

Hybrid breeds and crossbreeding

As we have learned, the Cockapoo is the product of crossing a Poodle with a Cocker Spaniel. This practice of cross-breeding isn't new, however some people who prefer purebreds are against it. The advantage of cross-breeding, and the reason it has become so popular in recent years is that it produces a dog that has the best qualities of two breeds. For example, among other traits, the Poodle has a low allergen coat, and the Cocker Spaniel has a gentle, affectionate personality. So, the resulting puppies of these breeds, when crossed, will produce a dog with both of these desirable qualities.

The first hybrid dogs

The first hybrid dogs, Labradoodles, were developed as guide dogs for blind people with allergies. At first, it was thought that the Poodle was completely hypo-allergenic but we now know that this isn't entirely true. Whilst they shed less fur and dander, they are not 100% hypo-allergenic. However, their low allergen qualities meant that they were used for a lot of experimental cross-breeding in the early days. The Labradoodle was heard of in breeding circles as far back as 1955, but it wasn't until the late 1980s that the hybrid breed became widely known.

First Cockapoos

The Cockapoo emerged in the USA in the 1950s, and along with the Labradoodle it is one of the oldest hybrid dog breeds. The breed was found to exhibit "hybrid vigour" which is associated with most cross-breeds, and means that there are far fewer health problems in the breed because of its mixed bloodline. It was cuddly and small like a house dog, yet it had the keen intellect and instincts of a working dog. Both the Poodle and the Cocker Spaniel have retriever and gun dog training in their heritage. However, the friendly, happy temperament of the Cocker balances out the more aloof traits of the Poodle, resulting in a dog that is easy to train and happy to meet new people and animals.

How does the Cockapoo's history affect its behaviour?

There are two ways that this little dog's heritage can affect its behaviour. Firstly, because the Cockapoo is a "designer" dog, it has been vulnerable to amateur backyard breeding in the past. The sudden demand for new hybrids like the Cockapoo led to a proliferation of breeders looking to make a quick buck. So, this means that whilst you will still enjoy many of the Cockapoo's favourable traits, if yours does not come from a good breeding line you could find yourself faced with more behavioural issues than you bargained for.

Secondly, and on the bright side, the Cockapoo's mixed heritage means that you are most likely going to get a dog that is intelligent, energetic and has a nice gentle temperament. With the strong gun dog and retriever heritage from both sides of the gene pool, you are going to need to keep your Cockapoo physically active or he will get bored, frustrated and may develop behavioural issues as a result. These dogs need mental stimulation and physical exercise in order to be happy. The good news is that this breed is relatively easy to train and loves to please, thanks to its long history of working closely alongside humans as hunting and retrieving companions.

Understanding your Cockapoo's temperament

Cockapoos are a firm favourite in the canine world. They're bright, energetic, and intelligent. This makes them fantastic family pets! However, there is far more to these little dogs than meets the eye. If you want to get a Cockapoo, you'll need to get a good idea of this breed's temperament and personality. Here are a few important things you should know.

Before you read on

One important thing to bear in mind with a hybrid dog like the

Cockapoo is that its temperament is going to depend heavily on the mix of Poodle and Cocker Spaniel that your pup came from. For example, if your Cockapoo's parents were a purebred Poodle and a Cockapoo, he is likely to have a temperament that is more like the Poodle than the Cocker. And vice versa.

With these hybrids, there can be a lot of variation in terms of appearance, and the same can be said for temperament. Always speak to your breeder and find out exactly which breeds are in your dog's bloodline, and spend some time with the pup's parents to see for yourself what kind of personality they might be passing down to their pups. Now that you understand this, we're going to explore the temperament of both the Cocker Spaniel and the Poodle, to lay the foundations for our understanding of the Cockapoo breed.

About the Cocker Spaniel temperament

Here are a few points to know about the purebred Cocker Spaniel's temperament. If you have a Cockapoo with more Cocker blood than Poodle blood, many of these traits might apply to him:

The Cocker is a very sociable dog. Not only has he been bred to enjoy the company of other dogs, he also craves human company, and like all gun dogs he likes to have a close bond with his master.

The Cocker has been bred with a strong urge to chase small animals, so if you have other pets this may not be a wise choice of dog for you. The Cocker's smaller size and his gentle persona make him an ideal companion for children. Just be careful that your child knows how to treat a dog and isn't too rough.

Cockers love to romp and play, and they will happily take a long hike or an ambling stroll with you for as long as you want. They have plenty of stamina and have a heritage of covering long distances back when they were hunting dogs. However, the good news is that they are relatively calm inside the home and are happy to settle down beside you in the evenings, after they have been walked and fed.

About the Poodle Temperament

Here are some points to know about the Poodle's temperament. If your Cockapoo has more Poodle in him than Cocker, you will probably recognise some of these traits:

Poodles are very trainable dogs, very active and inquisitive, mild mannered, good with children, but despite this they do make good family watch dogs as they are very protective.

They are also a very devoted and loyal breed with a good sense of fun. They do like to show off and this is why the French Circus used them in years gone by and they became very popular entertainers. The Standard Poodle has a much less excitable nature than its smaller cousins, the Toy and the Miniature, and is generally much quieter. They don't feel the need to take control of you so there will never be "leader of the pack" issues.

Miniatures live for affection, they are unlikely to want to rule your house, they are active, obedient and playful. Toys have exactly the same characteristics but can be little more nippy than the Miniatures and the Standards.

About the Cockapoo temperament

Now for the generic Cockapoo traits, which you can expect to see in a standard Cockapoo (a straight cross with a Cocker Spaniel and a Poodle, with no variations or other hybrids in the bloodline).

The Cockapoo is a sensitive soul

If you have a stressful house with feisty or unpredictable family members, you'll need to tone things down in order to welcome a Cockapoo into your household. These dogs can easily pick up on negative atmospheres and, like children, they can feel very unhappy when surrounded by unpleasant emotions. This sensitivity means that if you find yourself in a bad mood when you're about to start training your pup, you're better off postponing your training session until you feel

16

better. Positive vibes bring positive rewards!

Cockapoos are intelligent

It's fair to say that these dogs come with the intelligence of both the Poodle and the Cocker Spaniel, making them bright and alert. This makes them good candidates for agility training and for teaching tricks in your spare time. In addition, the huge advantage to this is that a new pup is going to be quite easy to house train. With some positive rewards and a bit of effort you should have them seeing the garden as their toilet in no time.

Cockapoos can get bored!

As with any of the more intelligent dog breeds, the Cockapoo likes to be kept busy. He needs a certain amount of mental stimulation to be happy. So, if he is left to his own devices for too long he will succumb to boredom, and this can be bad news for your home décor and furniture! There are some solutions to this: firstly, take your Cockapoo with you on errands and visits to friend's houses. They will thoroughly enjoy being where the action is! Secondly, give your dog plenty of walks, so that he is happy, calm and content. Thirdly, try not to leave your Cockapoo at home for long periods. If you're planning to be at the office for eight hours a day then you really shouldn't be thinking about getting a dog. They crave companionship and will be very unhappy without it. Later on in this book we'll look at behavioural problems caused by boredom in more depth.

Cockapoos are confident and happy

Generally speaking these little dogs are a happy-go-lucky breed who receive smiles wherever they go. They aren't the type of breed to be timid or fearful. On the contrary, they will be quite relaxed around strangers if raised in a happy household.

What Cockapoos need to be happy

These happy little dogs have an interesting heritage. On both the Poodle and the Spaniel sides, their ancestors were hunting dogs, responsible for sniffing out, fetching and retrieving game for their masters. Most of us know that the Springer Spaniel is a typical gun dog, but the Poodle was once known as a water dog, meaning it was trained to leap into the water and retrieve ducks and other game that had fallen there.

The name "Poodle" comes from an old German word "pudelin" which means to splash in water. Many people are often surprised that these smart, fashionable little dogs were once hard working retrievers! In light of this working heritage, here are some things the Cockapoo needs to have a happy lifestyle free from behavioural issues.

Agility and sports for Cockapoos

Cockapoos are great at agility training and they thoroughly enjoy a challenge! Agility training not only helps your Cockapoo to sue up all that excess energy, it also provides fantastic mental stimulation. Find out where your local agility club is online. You could also invest in some basic agility equipment for your garden if you want to have a go at training your dog from home.

Swimming

Both the Cocker Spaniel and the Poodle are excellent swimmers, so it's only natural that your Cockapoo will enjoy a paddle. Choose somewhere safe for swimming sessions – a lake with calm water and shallow shorelines is ideal. If you have a young pup, bear in mind that he might need a bit of training before he's confident in the water.

Sniffing and tracking

The natural urge to track scents is common in gun dogs and retrievers. The Cockapoo is no exception – he has a strong instinct to follow interesting scents and will absolutely love the chance to walk in the countryside where there are so many trails to be followed. At home, you can try hiding food in obscure places and letting him sniff out his snacks as he would do if he was still a gun dog.

Retrieving

Expert retrievers, Cockapoos will be eager to learn any form of fetch, even if it's just bringing you the newspaper! Buy plenty of toys and teach him to put them away after playtime. Outside, frisbee, ball games and retrieving sticks will also go down a treat.

Time off the lead

Time off the lead is essential for most dogs, but for the Cockapoo it's a must. These dogs have a heritage of roaming the countryside with their masters and they need a certain amount of freedom to indulge in these instincts, stretch their legs and follow scents. Before you try this, choose somewhere away from busy main roads and make sure your dog is fully trained to come when he is called.

Companionship

Gun dogs get on very well with other dogs, generally speaking. They will love the company of other dogs and the chance to make new acquaintances when out and about. This also holds true for human companionship – these working dogs bond closely with their masters and will not enjoy being left alone for long periods.

Now you know some of the most important ways to make your Cockapoo happy, it's time to go out and try them. These are excellent ways to avoid the many behavioural problems caused by boredom and frustration. Enjoy!

Understanding submissive or fearful Cockapoos

If your Cocka is fearful, submissive or prone to urinating when nervous, it's a sign he probably isn't as confident as he should be. A happy, well socialised Cocka should feel he is an important member of your family and should be calm in most situations. If he isn't then something needs to change. Here are some ways you can help.

How common is this behavioural problem?

Most well-bred Cockapoos are, by nature, happy and calm in most situations. However, due to the popularity of these little dogs and the desire to make a quick buck, some less-than-scrupulous breeders have unwittingly produced dogs with unfavourable traits. Over-submissiveness is one of these behavioural issues which can be found in certain bloodlines.

This is unfortunate as it ruins the fantastic reputation that the Cocka has as an excellent pet. To avoid getting one of the few Cockas with fearful or submissive traits, make sure you go to a good breeder who breeds for the love of the animals rather than purely for profit. Check that the pups have been raised in a relaxed and loving family environment. And always make sure you meet the parents of the pups so you can see for yourself what kind of personality they have.

Know the causes of submissive behaviour

A Cocka that is too submissive has what we humans would call a "low self-esteem". Some things that can cause this include:
- Being around overly-dominant dogs and having a "low ranking" in the doggy pack
- Too much scolding and punishment for bad behaviour
- A lack of praise and recognition for good behaviour
- Injuries and mobility problems, making him feel less able to escape when threatened
- Confinement in a crate for long periods of time (another form of punishment)
- Neglect and lack of contact with humans or other dogs

Familiarise yourself with the pack hierarchy

Today's domesticated dog is descended from the wolf. Wolves live in packs in the wild and they have a pack hierarchy where there is a dominant "alpha" male and lower ranking males. The alpha male gets to eat and mate first, and generally makes the pack decisions such as when to hunt and when to approach outsiders.

If your Cocka is overly submissive it means he believes himself to be ranking too low within your family pack. To a certain extent it is healthy for dogs to believe they rank lower than you do – it means they won't jump on the furniture or try to eat food from your plate. However, a balance needs to be struck or you will end up with a dog that is either over confident and dominant, or under confident and submissive.

Look for the signs of an overly submissive Cocka

You'll know your Cocka is too submissive if he:
- Urinates when stressed
- Can't be left alone without whining or crying
- Isn't confident with strangers and won't approach people to be petted
- Gets fearful with other dogs when out on walks
- Often crouches down or tries to make himself look smaller when meeting new people

Take action to boost your Cocka's self-worth

If you want a happy, confident and calm Cocka you will need to take action and make him feel loved and important. Here are some rules you should stick to:
- Lots of praise and affection is essential
- Treats help to show him he's loved
- Instead of reacting to bad behaviour such as urination, just ignore it (this tells your dog: "this behaviour serves no use whatsoever")
- Play lots of games to improve confidence – tug of war is a good one to let him win at!
- Lots of exercise should keep your Cocka calm and happy
- Keep your home as calm and happy as possible – Cockas are very sensitive and are affected by their home environments

Dealing with separation anxiety in Cockapoos

If your Cockapoo has been fussed over, spoilt or simply taken everywhere with you as a pup, he may grow up to develop a common Cocka behavioural problem: separation anxiety. This is where your dog cannot cope with being left alone, even for short periods, and develops a set of unhealthy behaviours caused by stress. For example, your Cocka might start to whimper and panic if he sees you grab your keys and put your coat on.

You might hear him barking or crying as you walk down the garden path. This can be very uncomfortable for owners to deal with – after all, who wants to leave their best friend whining and whimpering every time they go out? It's also not a nice way for your Cocka to have to live. Here are some ways to deal with it.

How to spot separation anxiety

When a dog has separation anxiety he may engage in the following behaviours:

- Urinating or defecating where he shouldn't
- Persistent barking or howling
- Chewing, scratching and otherwise destroying household objects
- Trying to escape from his confined space
- Pacing back and forth or in a circular motion
- Eating excrement

If your dog engages in these behaviours when you're nearby, then it is unrelated to separation anxiety and you will need to take steps to control this behaviour. If he is doing these things while he is alone, then it may be due to separation anxiety.

What has caused my Cocka's separation anxiety?

Separation anxiety is typically triggered by a change in the dog's living arrangements. For example, if he is given up to a shelter and then adopted by a family he may be more likely to have separation anxiety. Or, if you have previously spent a lot of time with your dog during the day, and then you suddenly get a job that requires you to be out of the house for long hours, then the change in your schedule may trigger separation anxiety.

The main cause of this anxiety is that, in the dog's mind, you are a member of his pack. In the wild, if a dog becomes separated from its pack he is usually much more vulnerable to predators, getting cold and not being able to hunt. So, he is naturally predisposed to want to be with you, wherever you go.

Add to this the Cockapoo's long history of being bred to accompany his master (and his fellow hounds) on long days of hunting, and you can see why separation anxiety is common in this very sociable breed.

Secondly, this issue is often caused by upbringing. A lot of the time, a dog with separation anxiety will not have been properly socialised as a puppy. This means he was never taught that it was OK to be alone. Maybe he had an owner that pandered to his every need, or that responded to every single cry for attention.

Maybe he has simply never been left alone before now. Lastly, dogs that were separated from, or rejected by, their mothers at a very young age are prone to separation anxiety, as well as dogs that have come from abusive homes.

What can I do for my anxious Cocka?

Here are some ways you can teach your dog to be more comfortable with spending time apart:

Repetition and reward

One of the main ways that dogs learn new behaviour is through repetition. So, you can begin by training your dog to get used to being alone for short periods. Put him in a room with his favourite toys and his bed, and leave him there for a while with the door closed. Don't make a fuss when you leave, just shut the door quietly and walk away. You should wait a few minutes before returning, and then give a treat and some praise.

Over a period of a few days, you can repeat this whilst gradually lengthening the amount of time you stay away. He will most definitely cry and whine at first, but will slowly get used to the idea of you leaving over time. He will also learn that you're always going to return before too long.

Practising the signals

Your dog probably picks up on the signs that you're about to leave the house, which is when the anxiety begins. These could include putting your coat on, putting on shoes, or the jingle of your house keys as you grab them. You can practice doing these things with him to get him more used to the idea. When he reacts badly, ignore him. When he stays calm and quiet, you can give him a reward. After a while he will learn that these trigger signals are not necessarily signs he is about to be left alone for long periods. They might be signs he is about to be praised or rewarded.

Make your exists calm and quiet

Avoid big goodbye cuddles when you leave, and don't make a big fuss. Ideally, you should leave with virtually no fanfare, through a door in a different room. Before you leave the house, ignore your Cocka for about 20 minutes so that when you're gone it doesn't seem like such a huge transition.

Leave the radio on

You can try leaving the radio or the TV on to see if this calms your Cocka down. Often the sounds and voices from the radio will stimulate his senses and make things seem a bit less silent after you've gone.

Plenty of w.a.l.k.s!

A well exercised dog is usually a happy and calm dog. If your dog has been walked before you leave the house, he's likely to be feeling calm, tired out and satisfied. Likewise if he's already been fed and has a nice full tummy.

Consider a canine companion

If you're spending long periods of time out of the house, perhaps because you're at work all day, then it might be worth considering another dog to keep your existing dog company. Dogs are, after all, meant to be pack animals and will naturally crave company. The reality is, you really should not have a dog if you're not there during the day to look after him.

If your Cocka is being left alone for hours at a time, why not get a dog-loving neighbour or friend to drop by and give him some attention. This could be walks, treats, or simply time hanging out. It will go a long way towards improving your dog's quality of life. There are also companies who offer doggy day care where your Cocka will get to meet lots of other canine companions.

Now that you've been given some handy tips for dealing with separation anxiety, it's time to try them out on your Cocka. Don't leave separation anxiety to resolve itself – this behavioural problem is a sign that your dog is genuinely stressed, and as a result it needs to be nipped in the bud.

You and your Cockapoo

Anthropomorphism

Anthropomorphism refers to the practice of attributing human characteristics to something other than a human, such as an object or animal. A common example of anthropomorphism is the Cockapoo owner who treats her canine pet as a human member of the family. This behaviour typically means that the dog is showered with an abundance of love and affection which, of course, is a wonderful thing. The bond we have with our pets can become very strong if we imagine that they are experiencing feelings and emotions similar to our own.

However, anthropomorphism can also be a destructive force when trying to establish healthy relationships between Cockapoos and their owners. In general, dogs tend to thrive when they are given rules and limitations. Setting clear boundaries for your Cockapoo's behaviour is essential in enabling you to live together in a safe and harmonious way.

Reminding yourself of the fact that your dog isn't a human (no matter how much he may act like one) will help you to understand why he behaves the way he does, and the steps you can take to modify his behaviour if necessary.

Language and relationships

Language is one of the most effective tools for developing a healthy relationship with your Cockapoo. Examples of the ways that you can use language to communicate with your dog include:

A strong tone of voice to assert your dominance and discipline. This is important to let your dog know that you make the rules and when his behaviour is unacceptable.

Key command words to train your dog to behave in a particular way. "Sit" and "stay" are common examples of these command words. Kind and affectionate language should be used to reward good behaviour and to demonstrate your love and happiness with your dog. A reassuring and comforting tone may be necessary if your dog is timid or scared.

Trust and respect

As with any healthy relationship, it is vital that a dog and its owner trust and respect each other. Your Cockapoo needs to trust that you will take care of his basic needs, not mistreat him, and give him the comfort and security he needs to live a healthy and happy life. You need to be able to trust that he is not going to harm you or other people or animals. You also need to be able to trust that he will behave appropriately around your possessions and in public places.

A big part of trusting your dog means being confident that he will obey your commands. Whether your Cockapoo chooses to obey you or not will depend upon whether he respects you as the dominant leader. Being clear and consistent with training, discipline and rewards will encourage him to respect your authority.

It is also important that you maintain a healthy level of respect for your dog. Keep in mind that some of your dog's behaviour is governed by animal instinct and that many of the situations he encounters in a domestic environment may be confusing or intimidating for him. This may cause him to behave in an unpredictable or undesirable way. Once mutual trust and respect has been established between you and your Cockapoo, the loyalty and unconditional love will flourish and you will develop an unbreakable bond.

Kindness, empathy and guidance

It goes without saying that all pets should be treated with kindness. It is arguable that kindness is particularly important for Cockapoos because of their loyal and companionable nature. Many Cockapoos demonstrate an unquenchable desire to please their owners. Rewarding their good behaviour with praise and love is vitally important for their health and well-being.

Empathy is also an important emotion to show towards your canine companion. Recognise that certain occasions may make him feel scared, insecure and uncertain. An urban environment can be a bewildering place for an animal and your Cockapoo will turn to you for guidance support in trying to understanding the world. Making an effort to empathise with him can help you to appreciate why he is behaving in a certain way and what you can do to help.

Survival instinct

Another essential factor in understanding your dog's behaviour is accepting that some of his actions occur due to an innate survival instinct.

As with other animals, dogs have evolved in accordance with the "survival of the fittest" principle. This manifests in modern domesticated dogs in a variety of ways. Possessiveness or aggression around their food, territorial behaviour in their home and barking when being approached by a stranger are actions that would have helped a wild dog to survive. When Cockapoos behave according to these instincts in a domestic environment it can be frustrating and potentially dangerous. Utilising the training techniques outlined later in this book can help you to improve your dog's behaviour.

Behavioural cycle

If you own a female Cockapoo then you will need to be aware of her ovulation cycle, as this can have a big impact on her attitude and behaviour. When females are in heat the hormone changes can cause her to become agitated and aggressive. This happens twice a year, for around three weeks at each time. Having your dog spayed can help to reduce or even eliminate these behavioural problems.

Behaviour and food

Whether your Cocka gets possessive around his food, or he begs at the dinner table, there are some techniques you can try to get him to behave around food. As with all other training and discipline issues, the key to building and maintaining good feeding habits in your Cockapoo is consistency. Establishing a set feeding routine will help him to learn that he can rely upon you, and that he needs to behave in an acceptable manner.

Consistency in feeding your Cockapoo means:
• having regular mealtimes

- always feeding him in the same location
- giving him a food bowl and water bowl that he can recognise as "his"
- making sure that he isn't interrupted while eating
- not feeding him scraps of food in the kitchen while you're cooking, or at the table while you're eating.

Consistency does not refer to the type of food that you feed your Cockapoo. As with humans, most dogs enjoy variety and will benefit from a diverse and nutritious meal-plan.

Priority feeding

Priority feeding is a training technique that is designed to teach your Cockapoo that you are in control of the food, and that he needs to respect you and your rules in order to receive it. It is based on the humans and the dog having separate meals, and the humans of the household having priority in the food receiving hierarchy.

It is recommended that you implement the following step-by-step process for two to three weeks with a new dog in order to establish good feeding habits:
1) Prepare your dog's meal and some food for yourself.
2) Eat a small amount of your food in your dog's view and then put his food bowl down on the ground. Don't say anything or make eye contact.
3) Walk away from the dog food, but stay nearby. If you leave the room then the dog may leave his meal and follow you.
4) If your dog walks away from the food bowl, then pick it up, whether the food has been eaten or not.
5) Ensure that your dog always has access to fresh, clean water.

Once your Cockapoo has learned that you control the food, and that he can trust you to feed him sufficiently, then you can stop the priority feeding system. You can always re-introduce this method again at a later date should he need reminding about good food manners.

Staying in control

If you don't want your canine companion to beg at the table when you are eating, or to steal food from the kitchen, then you need to stay in control of the food situation in your household. Relenting to your Cocka's begging, and feeding him from your meals, will send him a clear message that this behaviour is acceptable. This can then become a very difficult habit to break.

If your dog is persistently begging for food then you may need to take further steps to discourage this behaviour. Restricting access to these areas of the house at certain times is one effective step. It may also help to give him something else to occupy his time while the humans are eating, such as his own meal, a bone, or a chew-toy.

It's also important that you stay in control of the use of treats. Treats should only ever be used as a reward for your Cockapoo when they have obeyed a command or done something else that pleases you. Giving a dog treats for no reason at all reduces their effectiveness as a training aid and reward.

Food aggression

Some (not all) Cockapoos can be aggressive around food. It may be that they have experienced difficult conditions in the past in which they needed to fight for survival. Whatever the reason, food aggression can present a very dangerous situation for people or other animals that happen to be around the little dog while he is feeding.

If your dog displays aggressive behaviour around his food, it is important that you take action to reduce this danger and to make your home safer.

First, let's start with what NOT to do. If your Cockapoo is aggressive around food then don't leave food out for him at all times. He should only be fed at scheduled meal times and then once he's finished eating his bowl should be taken away, even if it still has food in it. Leaving it out can be confusing and unsettling for him as he thinks he needs to protect it all the time.

Don't yell at or punish your Cockapoo for food guarding. He is exhibiting a natural competitive instinct and you have to work with him to overcome it. Trying to dominate and overpower him may work against you as it could encourage him to become more aggressive. It may also cause him to distrust or fear you which can damage your relationship.

Carefully consider the safety of yourself, your family and any other people or animals when your Cockapoo is feeding. If he needs to be restrained on a leash, or isolated from others while eating, then this should be done until you feel confident that he can be trusted not to snap and bite.

When it comes to overcoming your dog's food aggression, your primary purpose is to make him relax and feel comfortable when people approach him while he's eating. Changing this attitude is a very gradual process that may take some weeks to complete. You should take it at a pace that you and your dog are comfortable with. Trying to rush through this process is counter-productive as it may result in your dog becoming stressed which will then trigger the aggression.

The method outlined below is based on convincing your Cockapoo that when someone approaches his bowl they may be bringing something much better and more exciting than what he's currently eating. This will help him establish positive connotations for people approaching him and will hopefully eradicate his fear and aggression.

Step 1
Put a bowl of dry kibble on the floor for your dog. Once he begins eating, stand a comfortable distance back from him and don't approach any closer. Talk to him in a calm, conversational tone and regularly toss a small treat towards him. The treat can be anything your Cockapoo really enjoys, such as beef, chicken, cheese or sausage.

He will probably turn his attention away from the bowl to get the treats. If he comes towards you for more treats, just ignore him and only start throwing them again once he returns to his bowl. Continue this method for a week or so, or until he seems at ease with this.

Step 2
Take all the same actions as in step 1 above, only this time move a step towards your Cockapoo each time you toss him the treat. After throwing the treat, step back to your starting position. Each day, begin a little bit closer to his bowl.

Continue this for a week or so, until he is comfortable with you standing around two feet away from him while he's eating.

Step 3
Put the bowl of dry kibble down for your Cockapoo and walk away. Once he starts eating, approach him using the same conversational tone and words that you have been using in the previous steps.

When you are standing right next to your dog's bowl, drop a treat into it and then walk away. Repeat this regularly until he finishes his meal. Do this for around two weeks or until your dog is completely comfortable with you approaching him while he's at his bowl.

Step 4
Put the dry kibble down as in previous steps. Approach your dog using the same language as before. When you're beside him, hold the treat out in your hand and bend down toward him. Tempt him to stop eating from the bowl and to take the treat from your hand. Repeat this process until he finishes eating. Continue this step for a week or two, getting closer to your dog each time.

Step 5
Continue the same actions as in step 5, except this time touch your Cockapoo's bowl with one hand while you're offering him the treat with the other hand.

Step 6
Begin as in step 5, but this time you want to pick the bowl up off the ground, drop the treat into it, and then return the bowl to the ground.

Start by only picking the bowl up a few inches off the ground, and then gradually increase the height until you are lifting it to your waist.

As you and your dog become more confident and comfortable with this routine, you can then begin to take the bowl to a nearby table or counter to put the treat in it before returning it to the usual spot on the floor.

The point of this exercise is for the dog to understand that if you take the bowl off him while he's eating, it will be returned to him with something better and more exciting in it.

The 6 steps outlined above are designed to give your dog positive mental associations with you approaching him when he's eating. This will help to ease or eradicate his food aggression. You will need to repeat this process with each member of your family feeding your Cockapoo to enable him to feel comfortable eating in front of every-one in the household.

Barking Cockapoos

There are many different reasons why a Cocka barks. It may be due to excitement, boredom, fear, loneliness, guarding its territory, or raising an alarm when something unusual is going on. Sometimes you may appreciate your little dog barking, for example if you want to be alerted when people are visiting your property. However, at many other times a Cockapoo's incessant barking can become an extreme annoyance for its owners and other people in the neighbourhood. Don't worry, there are ways to nip this in the bud.

Identifying why he is barking is the first step in controlling this disruptive behaviour. You may find that you are able to identify different types of barks – for instance, his "I'm excited and I want to play" bark will probably sound quite different to his territorial or warning bark. If you know what's causing the bark, then you can be more focused on trying to reduce it.

It's unrealistic to expect a dog to stop barking altogether; this is one of their primary means of communication. However, there are some steps that you can take to reduce your dog's barking in certain situations.

Barking at home – in the house

Barking in the house may be territorial or attention-seeking. He may also get very excited when people come to visit and barking is his way of greeting them. Whatever the reason, barking in the home can be annoying and off-putting for visitors, particularly if the dog is difficult to control.

If your Cockapoo is barking to get attention or a reward from you, such as play, a walk, a toy or food, then you need to take firm steps to show him that this behaviour is unacceptable. If you give him what he wants in response to his barking, then the lesson he learns is that barking is the best way for him to communicate and he will do it more and more often.

Barking in the garden

Your Cockapoo may be barking in the garden because he is territorial, bored, excited, communicating with other dogs in the neighbourhood, or trying to get your attention. Making sure that he has toys to play with, that he has a comfortable place to rest, and that he gets a lot of exercise and affection from you may help to reduce his barking outside. A large bone, or a chew-toy that he has to work at to release treats, can also help to distract him from barking for long periods of time.

If your dog is barking in the garden while you're at home, then bring him into the house and only let him outside when he has stopped barking. Repeat this behaviour whenever he barks. If he is jumping up at a window while inside and continuing to bark, then use a leash to secure him to a table or chair so that he can't see outside.

Barking on a walk

A dog barking on a walk could be an indication of excitement or alarm. If there is a trigger for his barking, such as when he is approached by a person, another dog, a bike or a car, then you can try to distract him during these moments to prevent the bark. Hold a treat in front of his nose and allow him to nibble at it while the thing that he would normally bark at is passing by. Praise him if he doesn't bark.

Dealing with excessive barking

The first step in dealing with excessive barking is to identify why your Cockapoo is barking in the first place. Think about when and where the barking occurs. What seems to trigger the barking? Does it only happen at a certain time of day or in a specific location? Once you understand the cause of the barking, then you can take steps to reduce it.

In some instances, the easiest cause of action in reducing your dog's barking will be to remove the triggers. If the dog can't see the things that are making him bark, then the barking will probably reduce. This may mean installing a fence that he can't see through, and restricting his access to the front door so he won't know when visitors are arriving.

Another way of dealing with excessive barking is to train your canine companion to be quiet on command. This requires a lot of dedication and patience, but it is well worth it as it will allow you to deal with all types of barking in a range of different locations and scenarios. This training method uses the reward system to teach your dog the meaning of the word "quiet" and to give you more control over his barking. When a barking trigger occurs (for example, a visitor arrives at your house), allow your dog to bark a couple of times and then say "quiet" calmly and confidently. Don't shout it as that will just suggest to your dog that loud noises are acceptable. Hold him by the collar with one hand and gently hold his mouth closed with your other hand and repeat "quiet". Once he has calmed down, let him go and ask him to sit beside you. Then reward him with a special treat. Encourage him to sit quietly beside you for a few minutes or until the trigger has passed by repeating "quiet" and frequently giving him more treats. Over time, he should learn that being quiet on command pleases you and gets him rewards.

Behaviour: Aggression

The potential for aggression is a very important factor when you are considering bringing a Cockapoo into your home to live with you and your family. Cockapoos, like most dog breeds, have sharp teeth and claws which can cause serious harm to people and other animals if they choose to attack. Dealing with any dog attack is a terrifying and devastating experience for all involved, and all possible steps should be taken to stop these horrible situations from occurring.

At the end of the day, you are responsible for your Cockapoo's behaviour. If he attacks someone, then you may face severe consequences. In some locations, dogs who act aggressively and who harm people or other animals, are required to be put down. This is why it's so important that you do all that you can to ensure that your four-legged friend isn't aggressive. Some of the risk factors associated with aggression include:

History

If you're adopting a Cockapoo from an animal shelter, then the shelter owners should be able to give you a good idea of the dog's history and temperament. Find out whether he ended up at the shelter due to behavioural issues, and ask what his temperament has been like at the shelter.

Age

It is usually easier to modify the behaviour of a younger dog than an older one. The saying that you "can't teach an old dog new tricks" is unfortunately quite true in this case. It can be extremely difficult to reduce aggression once it is present in an adult dog.

Severity

A dog may display some minor aggressive behaviour, for example, growling or showing his teeth, as a warning signal only and will not go any further. These less severe displays may make the dog easier to live with than dogs whose aggression is more severe. Of course, it can be very difficult to trust that the aggression will not get more severe in certain circumstances.

Triggers

Think about what triggers the Cockapoo's aggression and how easily these triggers are to avoid. If he only becomes aggressive if strangers act too familiar with him, then it may be easy to avoid these situations.

Aggression towards people

All dog owners need to be confident that their family, friends and visitors are safe from their dogs. If you have any fear that your dog may attack a person, then you should take all steps necessary to prevent this from happening. This may mean keeping your dog isolated from people by securing him on a leash, or keeping him outside when you have visitors in your home.

If your dog develops aggression towards people as he gets older, then it may be as a result of a medical condition. Speak to your vet to try to identify what might be the cause of his frustration and anger.
If your dog's aggression is particularly bad and you are not feeling

confident around him, then you might wish to seek advice from a professional dog behaviour expert. Someone with more experience in this field will be able to help you to understand what your canine companion is going through and suggest possible behaviour management techniques to help you deal with his aggression.

On-lead aggression

On-lead aggression, also known as leash reactivity, is a very confusing and frustrating behaviour because it is usually involves a Cockapoo who is normally calm and friendly turning into a cranky and aggressive terror as soon as he is on a lead. The dog's owners are usually puzzled as to how the nature of their beloved pet can change so much as a result of something so menial.

When you think of it from the dog's point of view however, it makes more sense. The lead is like a trap for him and so he is unable to investigate other dogs or people closely to work out whether they are a friend or foe. Without being able to make this assessment, the dog assumes the worst, and decides that he has to protect himself and his owner from potential threats. This is why he assumes an aggressive persona.

Possible solutions to this problem are:
- to walk at less busy times if possible,
- cross the road or turn around when you see another dog approaching
- ask your vet or pet store about different types of halters and leads that are specifically designed for on-lead aggression.

How to avoid being attacked

As a dog owner, you will probably be spending a fair amount of time around your own dog and other dogs. Visiting the park, walking, or even when visiting friends with dogs all present the possibility of being attacked. It may also be that the Cockapoo you have welcomed into your home has come from a rescue shelter and you may not have a complete understanding of his history. In any case, it is a good idea that you know how to avoid being attacked, or how to best handle yourself if an attack occurs.

The first rule to remember if you are confronted with an aggressive dog is to try to remain calm. Although this may be difficult in the situation, it is true that animals can sense fear and that this gives them more confidence in their own actions. Getting stressed or screaming may also make you appear more threatening which can provoke the dog further.

Secondly, you want to think about your body language. Don't run away as this draws on the dog's predatory nature and encourages him to chase and attack you. Instead stand completely still and avoid eye contact as he will see this as a challenge. Ignoring the dog and not responding to the aggression in any way increases the chances that he will simply lose interest in you and walk away.

If the threat continues, offer the dog something else to bite or chew on, such as a bag or drink bottle. If he gets distracted by something else, then you will hopefully be able to move away slowly.

Walking your Cockapoo is an essential way for it to get the exercise and stimulation he needs for an active and healthy life. It is particularly important if the dog is regularly confined in a small space with little opportunity for exercise.

Cockas were bred to have the stamina to roam long distances, and they need a good amount of exercise to burn off their excess energy. Walking your pet is also a great way to assist it with socialising and dealing with the rest of the world.

For all its benefits, dog walking can be extremely frustrating, painful and even dangerous if your dog doesn't behave the way you'd like him to whilst on the lead. Many Cockapoos become excited, boisterous and distracted while out for walks and this can make it a very stressful experience for the walker.

Why do Cockapoos pull?

The important thing to understand is that it is not a natural feeling for a dog to be constrained by a leash. Your Cockapoo wants to run and explore the exciting world, to sniff every tree, to chase every butterfly and to urinate on as many blades of grass as possible. In his mind, there is a lot to accomplish on the short time that he's out of the family home, yard or garden, and he mustn't waste a minute.

Unfortunately, for your four-legged friend, the world is not necessarily the safest place for him to go tearing about unrestrained. And for him to get the exercise he needs, it has to happen in a controlled and safe manner. That's why it's so important that you establish good walking behaviour with your dog as soon as possible.

It's a good idea for you and your Cockapoo to attend training classes together as the instructors will be able to give you helpful hints and guidance in learning to walk together in a safe, comfortable and relaxed manner. Ask your vet or pet store about dog behaviour classes in your local area.

If you're unable to attend a training class, then you will have to train your Cockapoo to walk properly on your own. It's important that you walk your dog at least once a day, and that you are consistent in your approach to training so that he learns the right way to behave. Maintaining a fast pace on your walks reduces the opportunities for your dog to get distracted by interesting smells you might pass along the way.

You might find it useful to tire your dog out a bit before taking him for a walk. Playing a game of fetch, or taking him to an off-leash area for a run, might make him less keen and energetic for your walk which will then make him pull less.

Silent correction

Disciplining your Cockapoo doesn't mean that you yell and scream at him when he does the wrong thing. In fact, this type of response can actually have a negative impact by confusing the dog, making him scared and potentially aggressive, not to mention being very stressful and negative for you. The main objective of discipline is to have your dog understand what actions are unacceptable, and have him refrain from doing certain things that you don't approve of.

A more effective discipline strategy is "silent correction". This method is based on you remaining calm and quiet, and thereby encouraging your dog to mimic this behaviour. It is a much more peaceful, and ultimately more effective, method of disciplining your pet.

There are 4 levels of silent correction that you can use in different situations with your Cockapoo. The appropriate level will depend upon the type of unacceptable behaviour that he is engaging in.

Level 1 – Turn away

If your Cockapoo is persistently nudging at you, jumping up on you, rubbing against you, or demanding your attention in some other way, then simply turning your face away from him should be sufficient to indicate that you are not interested in his demands and that he won't be rewarded with your attention by behaving in that manner. If he is jumping on you, then you may need to stand up and turn your whole body away from him. Don't say anything or touch him. The key is not giving him any recognition at all for behaving in this unacceptable way.

When he has calmed down and walked away from you, take some time and then, when you're ready, call him to you an give him a pat and a treat. This will help him to recognise that he needs to respect your space, but that you still love him and will give him affection at a time that suits you.

Level 2 – Guide and hold away

If you have tried the "turn away" response mentioned above and your Cockapoo hasn't taken the hint and is persisting in trying to get your attention, then you will need to be more assertive. It's important that you don't respond emotionally (even if you are getting annoyed), that you don't speak to your dog, and that you don't make eye contact. All of these actions send mixed messages to your dog as they show him that he has got your attention and that he has therefore succeeded in his mission.

Instead, you need to remain calm and firmly guide the dog away from you. Hold him by the collar at an arm's length distance from you until he has relaxed and then let him go. If he comes back to you, then simply repeat the "guide and hold away" motion until he has stopped. If he continues to bother you, then level 3 may be required.

Level 3 – Guide and walk away

This response can be used in a variety of situations where your Cockapoo is doing something that you don't want him to do. For example, if he is persistently jumping up on you or a guest, or if he is climbing on furniture.

As soon as you see him doing something that you find unacceptable, then you need to intervene so that he knows that behaviour is not allowed. You also need to be consistent in enforcing these rules so that your dog gets a clear message about what he can and can't do.

Again, with level 3, you should remain calm, silent and refrain from making eye contact with your Cockapoo. You need to quietly walk to your dog, take him by the collar, turn him around 180 degrees from the area that he was interested in (whether it be a person, piece of furniture or something else) and walk him away.

If convenient, you may choose to take him to his bed, but any quiet spot away from the area of interest will do. Hold him there for a few seconds until he relaxes and then walk away. You may need to repeat this several times until the offending behaviour ceases.

Level 4 – Time Out

This final level can be used if the previous 3 levels haven't worked, or if your dog has done something that is completely unacceptable, such as biting or jumping on children. The objective here is showing your dog that if he does these things he will be left alone. If practical, then you and your guests should walk out of the room you're in and close the door behind you leaving him on his own.

Leave him for about 15 seconds, and then walk back in. Once you're ready, call him to you and acknowledge him, only if he comes to you on your terms.

If he jumps on you or your guests when you re-enter the room, then walk out again and double the amount of time that you leave him alone for. Keep doing this until he calms down.

Remember, that the key to the silent correction method of discipline is to remain calm and unemotional without speaking to or looking at your dog. The bad behaviour that he's doing (particularly if it's jumping up on people) is to get attention from you, and by giving him attention you are teaching him that that behaviour is acceptable. When he understands that changing his behaviour gets a reward from you then you will have a dog with much better manners.

Basic commands

This section will go through some useful basic commands for you to teach your Cocka. Once your dog is fully trained, it will be a lot easier to take him everywhere with you and introduce him to new people and situations. It is well worth the effort, so be persistent!

Sit and lie down

Learning to sit on command is usually one of the first skills that an owner teaches a dog. It is an important tool for behaviour and control issues, and it is a relatively easy trick for the dog to learn.

Lying on command can help you to assert control over your dog as he is unable to do all manner of naughty things (jumping up, chasing things, begging at the table or running out the door) if he is lying down. It is a good way of controlling his impulsive nature which can help to protect him and others.

It's a good idea to teach your dog to sit first, as the process for teaching lying down begins in the sit position.

Teaching your Cockapoo to sit

Step 1
Stand in front of your dog and say "sit" in a loud and clear voice. Hold a treat in your hand about an inch away from your dog's noise.

Step 2
Slowly move your hand and the treat up towards the top of your dog's head. When this happens your dog will usually follow the treat with his eyes and then his nose. This movement will cause his rear to go to the ground and into a sitting position.

Step 3

Once she is sitting, say "Yes!" and give the treat. Repeat these 3 steps several times.

Step 4

The next step is to get your dog to sit without the lure of the treat in your guiding hand. Leave the treat in your pocket and follow the first 3 steps outlined above with just your empty hand guiding your dog's movement. When he sits, give him the treat from your pocket as a reward.

Step 5

Next, you want to remove the hand signal. You can do this by gradually reducing the amount of movement you make with your hand. Start by holding your hand around 10 inches or so from your dog's face when saying "sit".

He will probably be sufficiently accustomed with the verbal command and the anticipated reward that he will sit immediately, but if he doesn't then make a small movement with your hand over his head. This should be the prompt needed for him to drop to sitting. As before, continue to give him a treat whenever he sits on command.

Teaching your Cockapoo to lie down

Step 1

Ask your dog to "sit". Once he is in the sitting position, give the command "down".

Step 2

Holding a treat between your fingers in front of your dog's nose, slowly lower your hand down towards the floor, between your dog's front legs. This will encourage your dog to bring his head down to the floor. When your hand is touching the floor between your dog's front paws, slowly move it in a straight line away from your dog. This will encourage your dog to bend his elbows and drop into the lying position.

Step 3

Once he is lying down, say "Yes!" and give him the treat. Move away and encourage him to get up out of the lying position. Repeat these steps about 15 times over several days until your dog seems comfortable with this new skill.

Step 4

The next step involves using a simple hand gesture, without a treat, to lure your dog into the lying position. Once again, start with your dog in the "sit" position and then say "down". Lower your hand (without a treat) towards then ground in the same motion that you used previously to guide your dog's head and body to the ground. When your dog is lying on the ground say "yes!" and give him a treat as a reward. Repeat this regularly for a couple of weeks until your dog begins lying down as soon as you use the cue and hand signal.

Step 5

Gradually reduce the hand signal into a small and then smaller movement. Eventually you want to simply be giving the command "down" while pointing at a position on the floor.

Step 6

The real usefulness of this command is being able to get your dog to lie down to prevent him from misbehaving or getting into a dangerous situation. For example, when guests arrive at your house, having your dog lie down on command can prevent him from jumping up and annoying or injuring them. Therefore, the next step in your dog's lying down training is teaching him to lie down when there are distractions.

The trick here is to introduce the distractions gradually. Don't start off by expecting him to lie down on command when someone knocks at the door, or when another dog comes running up to him. These are exciting situations for him and expecting him to respond to his training immediately in these situations is setting him up to fail.

Start by simply varying the times and locations of your training sessions. Try each room in your house, different places in your yard and different times of the day. Then introduce gradual distractions, such as busier places in your home where family members are walking about and talking, or while you're on a walk or at the park. Then try using the command when people knock on your door or ring your doorbell.

Continuing to use treats as a reward is a good idea, but you might want to gradually phase these out as you probably won't have treats on hand every time you want your dog to respond to your commands. Using another type of reward for good behaviour, such as a cuddle, game or walk, can be an effective substitute.

Fetch

Playing fetch is a classic way of interacting with your dog. It is also a great form of stimulation and exercise that many dogs really enjoy. Some dogs get so much enjoyment from this simple game that you may find it hard to bring the game to an end!

There are many different items that you can play fetch with, such as a tennis ball, a frisbee, a stick, a toy or some other specifically designed dog ball. Experiment with different items to see if your dog has a preference. Make sure that the item isn't small enough for your dog to swallow, or too hard that it might chip your dog's teeth.

If your dog doesn't seem to understand the concept of chasing after and retrieving an item, there are some simple steps that you can take to introduce him to this game. If your dog likes playing tug-of-war then start with this game and once you've worked the toy out of his mouth toss it a short distance away from you. If he runs to get it, then you immediately grab it too and start playing tug-of war again. Gradually start throwing the toy further away from you until your dog has to run for it. Encourage him to bring it back to you by playing a quick game of tug-of-war with him each time he returns.

Some dogs will be really keen to chase after a toy, but they don't seem interested in returning it to you. A good response to these situations is the "bait and switch" technique. For this to work, you will need to have two identical toys to use. When your dog is excited and ready to play, show him one of the toys, throw it for him and encourage him to fetch it using a "go get it" or similar type of command.

He'll probably run after the toy, pick it up, and then look back to see what you're doing next. At that point, show him the second toy and pretend to throw it away from your dog. This will probably cause your dog to drop the first toy and come running towards you to chase after the second toy. Throw the second toy for him and while he's chasing after it go and get the first toy. Repeat this sequence for a week or 2. This will get your dog used to chasing a toy, picking it up and then running back to you.

Once this has been mastered, you can then try to phase out the second toy. Throw the first toy as before, and then call your dog once he's picked it up. Don't show him the second toy. Hopefully, he will keep the first toy in his mouth when he comes running back to you. When he's close to you show him the second toy and at the same time say "drop it". Seeing the second toy should make him drop the first toy. Throw the second toy for him and repeat. Gradually, he should learn the meaning of "drop it" and then you can phase out the second toy altogether.

Mouthing

"Mouthing" refers to the way a puppy, or sometimes an older dog, chews on or closes its jaws around part of a person's body. As a puppy, mouthing begins as little nips and nibbles, but as the dog gets older and his jaws get stronger this can turn into a serious bite.

It's important that you establish early on with a new puppy that mouthing is unacceptable. If a puppy (under 16 weeks of age) mouths you, then you should show that you are unhappy with this behaviour by yelling "Ow!" and walking away from him.

Smiling dogs

Bearing their teeth is generally an indication of fear and aggression in dogs, however, some dogs have actually learned to show their teeth in a smile. They have seen their human companions making this type of face when happy, and they have learned to copy the expression. Of course, doing this usually provokes a positive response from the people around them, so the dog continues doing it. It's a cute, although somewhat strange, way that our dogs are trying to please us. It's nothing to worry about!

Barging through doorways

Some dogs seem to have a natural instinct to barge through a door as soon as it's opened. There are many reasons why your dog may want to do this, including:
- a desire to explore the outside world
- looking for a mate (if they haven't been neutered)
- fear of something inside.

Barging through doorways is a behaviour that should be eliminated as quickly as possible because it is unsafe for people trying to come through the door and for the dog itself. In its excitement and haste to get through the door, the dog may dart out into the path of oncoming traffic or some other threat.

The best way of dealing with this problem is by teaching your dog to sit or lie down whenever a door is opened. If you're finding it difficult to stop this habit, then please ensure that your dog is micro-chipped or at the very least has a collar tag with your contact details on it. This will enable you to be contacted should the dog get lost or end up in an animal shelter.

Jumping up

Many Cockapoos like to jump up on people as a form of greeting. This can be quite a sweet display of affection as the dog is simply trying to be close to his human companion's eye level for the best opportunity to say hello. Unfortunately, because dogs can be heavy, dirty and boisterous, many people don't appreciate being jumped on by a dog.

The important thing to remember when trying to eliminate this type of behaviour is not to reward your dog with the attention that he is looking for. You need to make him understand that the appropriate way to greet a human is with all four of his feet on the ground. This means that if your dog jumps up on you when you enter the room, the best course of action is simply to ignore him.

Don't look at him, touch him or speak to him. When he realises that jumping up isn't going to get him the attention that he is craving, his feet will return to the floor. This is when you should shower him with love and affection to reinforce the notion that not jumping is the behaviour you're looking for.

On-lead pulling

Walking on a lead is not a natural situation for a dog; it's something that they need to be taught. Optimal lead behaviour has the dog walking beside its owner, not pulling ahead or trying to run off, and not lagging behind and stopping to sniff every pole and tree it passes. Teaching good walking manners takes a lot of time and dedication.

Chasing other animals

Some dogs seem to have a natural instinct to chase other animals, whether it be out of curiosity, excitement, or a more predatory desire. This behaviour needs to be strongly discouraged as it is potentially harmful for both the dog and for the animal being chased. If your dog is wildly pursuing another animal, then it may be distracted from other threats to its safety, such as traffic. Also, the other animal may scratch or bite your dog leading to injury or infection.

If your dog has a tendency to chase domestic or wild animals, then it is your responsibility to make sure that he is securely contained inside your house or garden, or that he is on a lead when you take him outside your property. You should also train your dog to come to you when he is called so that you are able to exert some level of control over him should he escape from your home or lead.

Marking

Urine marking is common behaviour for both male and female dogs. Dogs do this when they smell another dog's urine in their regular environment, which includes any place that he frequently visits. It is a way that they can communicate information about themselves to other dogs who sniff the urine. Dogs who haven't been spayed or neutered tend to urine mark more than those who have been.

Avoiding play

It's important to understand that, like humans, Cockapoos each have their own unique personalities. Some may be extremely playful, energetic and excitable. Others may be more relaxed, laid-back and lazy. While you can encourage your dog to play with you as much as you like, some dogs just may not be that interested in playing.

If your dog is avoiding play, there are a few things that you should consider. Possibly he is getting old. Dogs start to lose some of their energy and become less interested in play as they age. Consider whether there is possibly something medically wrong with your dog. Are they healthy and happy?

A visit to the vet may be required to rule out any medical conditions. Does your dog have enough stimulation and interest? Provide your dog with plenty of toys, exercise and opportunities for play.

Tail chasing

Tail chasing may seem like a funny and harmless activity at first, but if it's encouraged it can turn into a compulsive disorder resulting in exhaustion or injury. A small amount of tail chasing is fine for puppies as they are discovering the parameters of their own body and how they are able to move. However, if your dog continues to chase its tail a lot into adulthood, then you should take steps to reduce this behaviour.

Firstly, make sure that your dog is getting a sufficient amount of exercise. He may be chasing his tail out of boredom or to burn off excess energy. Exercising him more may solve the problem by leaving him too tired and relaxed to bother with his tail. Providing him with chew-toys and other entertainment will also serve as a distraction from chasing his tail.

If the problem continues then distraction is the best way of dealing with it. Offer your dog a game, a walk, or a treat as soon as you see him beginning to chase his tail. Hopefully, if he is distracted often enough, then he will completely forget about his habit of chasing his tail.

Digging up the garden

There are many reasons why your dog may seem determined to dig up your garden. He may be trying to create a cool and comfortable place to rest. He may want to bury a treasured item, such as a bone or toy. Or he may simply be doing it because he finds it fun. Whatever the reason for his digging, this can be a very annoying habit, especially if you are a keen gardener and like to have your garden a particular way.

Your strategy for stopping the digging is determined by the reason why your dog is digging in the first place. Maybe your dog is too warm or too cold, and he needs a more comfortable place to rest during the day. Allowing him to stay inside during extreme weather, or providing him with shade, shelter or a comfortable bed, may make a difference.

If your dog is burying items then try not to give him treats that he won't finish completely in one go. Or, if he doesn't finish a bone or a chew toy, try to get it off him once he's finished with it and then give it back to him again later. Just don't leave it with him.

A dog who digs for fun presents a more difficult problem and it may not be possible to eliminate this behaviour completely. Instead you should direct your energy into trying to minimise the damage caused by the digging. Fence off any particular areas of your yard or garden that you'd like to protect. You may also wish to provide your dog with a digging pit and encourage him to dig in this area only.

Noise Anxiety

Your Cockapoo may demonstrate that he's afraid of noises by displaying some or all of the following symptoms – panting and drooling, whining, avoidance or attempting to run away or escape in response to a loud or unusual noise.

A dog may also 'learn' to be afraid of a particular noise, for instance, if it is associated with a painful or scary experience. For instance, if a dog's tail is caught in a slamming door, then he may develop a fear of the sound of slamming doors in the future.

As with other phobias in dogs and humans, there are different levels of seriousness and whether you choose to do anything about your dog's noise anxiety should depend upon whether you see it as being detrimental to his well-being or quality of life. In less serious instances, simply avoiding the sound as much as possible and then comforting your dog when the noise occurs may be the most practical response.

If your dog's noise anxiety is more extreme then further treatment may be required. You may find that distraction or comfort may be sufficient, for example, if your dog is scared of storms then playing a game or cuddling with him during a storm may be enough to calm him down.

However, remember that attempting to reassure the dog with a cuddle can have the opposite effect and make your dog think that there is actually something to be scared about. If your dog gets really distressed, then it is a good idea to speak to your vet about possible solutions to this problem.

Bottom shuffling

It can be quite an awkward and embarrassing sight to see your beloved Cockapoo dragging its bottom across the carpet or grass, however there are several reasons why your dog might be doing this, and it's not a laughing matter. Bottom shuffling usually occurs because there is a source of irritation or pain in that region, and your dog is trying to find relief. You can help by taking your dog to the vet to identify and treat the source of the problem.

The most likely causes of irritation causing bottom shuffling are:

Problems with the anal glands. The anal glands are located on either side of the dog's anus and sometimes these glands can become blocked, inflamed or abscessed.

 If your dog has a problem with his anal glands then he may be finding it difficult to defecate, he may try to bite or lick the area, it may be swollen and he may be bottom shuffling. Your vet can easily treat anal gland issues either by prescribing antibiotics if there is an infection, by expressing the glands (squeezing out the contents if they're too full), or recommending a change in diet.

Worms. dogs with tapeworms will also bottom shuffle to try to relieve the itchiness of the worms. If this is the cause of the shuffling then the worms will also be visible around your dog's anus. The best cause of action when it comes to worms is prevention, and you should speak to your vet or dog-breeder about worm prevention medication. If your dog has worms, then your vet can administer medication to treat it.

Faecal contamination. Diarrhoea and constipation can both cause the hair around your dog's bottom to become dirty and matted. This can lead to discomfort which your dog responds to by bottom shuffling. This situation is easily treated by washing the area and trimming away any matted hair. Make sure to check whether the skin his become infected. If so, you should seek treatment from your vet. If your dog is constipated or has diarrhoea for more than a day or 2, then you should also visit your vet.

Eating faeces

As disgusting as it sounds to us, eating their own or another animal's faeces is a normal behaviour for dogs. This behaviour is known as coprophagia, and although it is most common in puppies and nursing mothers, it can occur in other adult dogs. There is little explanation for this strange behaviour, although if the dog is an impoverished environment lacking in nutritional food or a sufficient amount of food, then coprophagia is likely to be more common.

If you want to stop your dog from eating faeces then some things to try include:
• ruling out any dietary deficiencies. Your vet may be able to assist with this if you're not sure what you're looking for.
• be vigilant with cleaning your yard and your cat's litter tray (if applicable) of faeces as soon as you're able to.
• train your dog using a "leave it" cue and reward system.

Mounting

Mounting is a normal dog behaviour that is often hard to avoid. You may find your Cockapoo mounting and thrusting up against a toy, a chair, another animal or even a person. Puppies learn to do this as they reach sexual maturity and then dogs continue doing it because they have learned that it feels good. It will typically happen when they get so excited in response to play, either with another dog or a person, that they are unable to control themselves.

If your dog's mounting behaviour isn't too often (no more than once or twice a day) and it's not bothering you, then there's no reason to try to stop this behaviour. If, however, your dog is mounting excessively, or the mounting has the potential to harm another person or animal (for instance, a large dog trying to mount a small child), then you should take steps to reduce or eliminate this behaviour.

It's also worth noting that some dogs don't appreciate being mounted, and your dog may find himself in trouble if he mounts an aggressive dog who doesn't like it. Teaching your dog to leave other dogs alone may be necessary for his own safety.

If your Cockapoo hasn't yet been neutered or spayed,tPanting, licking, prancing and pawing the object are typical signals that the dog is feeling amorous and is about to mount. Being on the lookout for these signals means that you will usually be able to distract your dog (with a toy, a game or a trained command like 'sit') before the mounting happens.

Behaviour with children

Bringing a dog home can be a very anxious experience for parents. While having a pet is a great experience for children, and one which teaches them a lot about responsibility and companionship, there is no hiding the fact that pets can be unpredictable and it's possible that your dog might be dangerous. You need to carefully monitor and continuously reassess whether or not your children are safe around your dog.

A big part of this is ensuring that your child treats your dog kindly and respectfully. Young children should always be supervised around animals as they may unintentionally frighten or be too rough with your dog. If you're unable to supervise your dog and child, then they should be separated.

When a Cockapoo is hurt or startled, he may respond with a growl or a snap. This can be frightening for the child and parent, however, it is usually just the dog trying to establishhis own boundaries. Many dogs will tolerate an amazing amount from a child, but there are some limits.

At the same time, the child needs to be taught the right way to treat an animal. You should also teach your child that, even if her pet dog at home is kind and loving and patient with her at all times, not all dogs are as reliable. Kids need to understand that they shouldn't approach and pat dogs that they don't know in the park or street without the owner's permission.

Another potential problem with dogs and kids are the dogs who love kids but are too large or high spirited to play with them appropriately. These types of dogs need to be trained not to ever jump up on people. Teaching your dog to sit or lie down on command can be effective ways of calming him down when there are children around.

Early Puppy Training

Bringing home a new Cockapoo puppy is an exciting event for the whole family. It is also exciting for your new furry friend. He needs to learn the rules of your house, though before he begins making rules by himself that may not please you.

Housebreaking

There have been many books and blogs written on housebreaking puppies, and many will have ideas that you can incorporate into a successful house-training program for your new puppy.

When you housebreak your puppy, it is essential to reward him when he goes to the toilet (eliminates) in the place you want him to, which is usually outside the house. At the same time, he must learn that doing so inside the house is not acceptable.

Crating is sometimes used in housebreaking, but it is better to keep confinement time to a minimum. Some puppies learn very easily where they can eliminate and where they cannot. Others will take longer to learn. By the time your puppy is four or five months old, he will probably be trained, and possibly well before that.

It is not unusual for a puppy to catch on for a while and then go backwards, either. Puppies do not have excellent bladder or bowel control when they are young. Your puppy may understand that he needs to go outside, but not yet be physically capable of always controlling his growing body.

How Often Should You Take Your Puppy Out?

Cockapoo puppies are all unique individuals, but most can only hold their waste for the number in hours that they are months old. Therefore, a six-month old puppy may only be able to go six hours without having a chance to go outside. He will usually be able to hold it better at night, since he is not drinking or eating and is usually inactive.

Steps in Housebreaking

1. Take your puppy outside on a schedule that is consistent. Every hour is a good starting point, and a short time after naps, playtime and meals. Your puppy will need to go out the first thing each morning, right before he goes to sleep at night and before you crate him or leave him alone in your house.

2. Maintain the same feeding times each day and do not leave food out between his meals.

3. In between the times you are taking him out, keep an eye on him.

Watch for any signs that he needs to go to the bathroom, so that you can anticipate the need and help him get outside before he has an "accident". Signs your puppy may show when he needs to go out include circling, whining, sniffing, pacing or leaving the room.

Take your puppy outside as soon as you can if you see one or more of these signs. Not all puppies will learn to let you know by scratching at the door or barking when they need to eliminate. Some may pace a little and then go to the bathroom inside the house.

4. If you cannot be home to watch your puppy, you should confine him to a small room or a crate. If he has his own room that you leave him in, close the door or use a baby gate to block the exits.

5. As he becomes more housebroken, your puppy can be given more freedom, with a larger room or multiple areas within the home. After he goes to the toilet outside, allow him some free time in the house and then place him back into his small room or crate. As he becomes more consistent, the times of confinement can be shortened.

6. Go outside with your puppy and give him a reward when he eliminates outside. Praise him, take a walk with him or give him a treat. Take him to the same area every time he goes out. He will smell the "purpose" of the area and understand what you expect him to do. Your puppy may eliminate when you first take him out for a walk, but others play and move about more before they eliminate.

7. If you catch your puppy eliminating inside the house, clap twice, to startle him but not to scare him. If he stops in mid-steam, take him quickly outside. You may have to use his collar to run outside with him. If he finishes eliminating in the yard or designated area, reward him with lots of praise and perhaps a treat.

8. If your puppy does not eliminate when he does get outside, he may have been finishing up when you caught him in the act. Watch him a bit more closely when he is inside.

If your puppy has an accident in your house, and you find it after the fact, do not correct him. He will not connect your punishment with an accident he had hours ago, or even minutes ago.

Crate Training

You may wonder why your puppy likes to snuggle under chairs or in tight spaces. Dogs are naturally adapted to live in dens, and they look for spaces that feel like a den to them. A dog crate is an excellent den, and can give your puppy a secure and safe environment that he will not mind going to at all.

Crate training is the most effective and quickest way to housebreak puppies. Your puppy's natural instinct is to avoid his own waste, so he will try very hard not to eliminate in his crate.

Selecting a Crate

Choose a crate that has room for your puppy to stand in, and to stretch out in. If you buy one that is too big for him, he can still sleep in one end and eliminate in the other, which defeats the object of using the crate to housetrain. If you want one crate to last into his adulthood, select one with a divider panel to use when he is still small.

Place your puppy's crate in the living area during daytime hours, so he can be with you and your family, if you have one. Put his crate in your bedroom at night if possible, so that he can sleep near you, since you are part of his "pack". This gives you an opportunity to correct your puppy if he fusses while he is in the crate.

When you release your dog from his crate, take him outside right away. Encourage him to eliminate while he is out and praise him when he does. Supervise him whenever he is in the house if he is not totally housebroken yet.

Keeping Your Puppy on a Schedule

If you maintain regular feeding times with your puppy and use his crate as outlined here, you should have a puppy that is happy in his crate, when you need him to remain there.

If your puppy likes to chew things to the point of being destructive, especially when unsupervised, anxious or bored, you can use a crate when you are away for eliminating this habit. Your dog probably sleeps most of the time you are at work anyway, so crating him gives him a den, while it protects your furnishings from chewing. It also prevents your puppy from eating anything that might harm him.
If your puppy experiences separation anxiety when you are leaving home, this is because he is a pack animal. He does not deal well with isolation, and he does not know when you will return. Giving your dog a positive experience with crating helps to remedy his separation anxiety.

The crate should never be used for punishment. It should be a place where your dog enjoys spending idle time.

If you will be travelling with your dog, he will need a crate. Preparing him when he is still young gives him a positive experience and ensures less stress while travelling. When you properly train your puppy, he will not resent the crate, and it will become a sanctuary for him.

Advanced Puppy Training

How to Nip Nipping in the Bud

Even the friendliest Cockapoo puppy will sometimes nip you or your family. He gets attention when he does this, and he may be teething, too. Most puppies grow out of this habit, but you do not want to use over-correction while it is still occurring.

Teach your new puppy by reacting with an "ouch" when he bites a bit too hard. As he discovers that people are sensitive to his nipping, he should respond in a positive way and stop with most of the nipping. When puppies nip, they are usually playful. Make sure your new friend has plenty of dog-safe chew toys at his disposal. Play with him only when he is being gentle with you.

You may also keep a toy with you as a substitute for nipping your hand, but it cannot feel like a reward to the puppy when you substitute a toy, or he will be getting positive reinforcement instead of you asking him to change this behaviour.

Be sure your puppy gets plenty of exercise, to use up all that extra energy he has. He should also get solid rest time, at least 12 hours a day. Chew toys need to be readily available for your dog, when he wants to chew.

Playing with dog Toys, Not Furniture or Collectibles

It is natural for dogs to chew, but you don't want your puppy wrecking expensive items in your home. Your dog may chew when you are away, too, if he is anxious because you are gone.

Lonely dogs may chew because they are bored. Give your dog plenty of exercise when you are home, so that he'll be tired and sleep more readily when you are away. You may also give him a place that is his alone, like a kennel or a crate. You can use a small room like your second bathroom, if you want to give him more room. This assumes that he is already housebroken and doesn't need a crate for that reason.

When your dog shows a love for chewing things he shouldn't, keep him crated while you are away. Give him several chew toys that are safe for him even while you are not there to supervise him. This means toys that cannot be easily consumed. Kong Toys with food or treats in them work well, but many toys come with a warning that dogs should not play with them unless they are supervised.

Don't give your puppy old towels or shoes to play with. He doesn't know the difference between old and new items, and you will be inadvertently telling him it's OK to chew on your new shoes, too.

When you leave your home, put your puppy in the area you have selected for his confinement and give him several safe chewies. Avoid long good-byes, because those may tend to make him more anxious. Just tell him that you'll see him later and head on your way.

Give your puppy as few opportunities to chew foreign objects as you can, which means confining him whenever you leave. As he becomes more predictable, you can place him in his crate with the door left open. Leave the house for 10 or 15 minutes and check for any chewed objects when you return.

If your dog seems overly anxious when you leave the house, he may have separation anxiety, which can also lead to chewing. He is a pack animal and he worries when you're gone.

Select a meat-scented bone made from nylon, which will be safe for him when you're not home. Play with your puppy and this bone a few times every day. The bone will be more interesting for him not just because of the meaty scent, but because of your scent, as well.

You can help an anxious dog to adjust the same way that you would a lonely dog, but it may take more time to accomplish the goal of not chewing on something he shouldn't. Slowly increase his alone time crated with the door open, so that he can adjust to your being out of the house, without feeling so anxious.

You are the Alpha dog

As a responsible dog owner, you need to be sure that your puppy knows his rightful place in your pack of humans. Your puppy may initially growl at humans when eating, or guard his food. You need to establish from day one that you are the alpha dog. The puppy cannot be allowed to take your place. When your puppy knows his place in the household pack, he will be happy and better adjusted. He will not be confused or suffer as much separation anxiety, and he won't display unwanted behaviour due to not knowing where he stands in the pack.

Communicating with Your Cockapoo that You Are the Pack Leader

Taking your puppy for a walk is the easiest way to let him know you are the leader of the pack, and that this pecking order will not be changed with his addition to the house. In a walk that teaches pack rule, your puppy must walk beside you or behind you. In his mind, the pack leader is always in front. If your dog is always pulling you when you walk, he is trying to take your place as the natural pack leader.

Your puppy should be beside you or following you, rather than trying to lead you. A daily pack walk will release his pent-up energy and satisfy his migration instincts.

Feeding Time – Humans First

All the people in your house should eat before your puppy does, since the leader in a pack always has his fill before the rest. If it's time for a puppy meal but not one of your own, eat a small snack before you give him his meal. This reinforces the fact that the pack leader eats first.

Do not feed your puppy table scraps while you eat a meal. Feed your dog at a consistent, scheduled time. You choose the time, not him.

Movement in the Home

If you and your puppy are going upstairs, you should go first. The same thing is true with moving from one room to another or going through doorways. You must always proceed before your dog. If your puppy does not catch on right away, have him sit and then allow him to come after you have gone past.

Greeting Guests

You should greet your guests before your dog does so. He should be the last one to get attention, in deference to humans as pack leaders. If your puppy happens to be lying down between you and wherever you are headed in the house, step over him or ask him to move. Never change your route to go around him, or you are deferring to him.

Eye Contact

If your dog tends to be dominant, eye contact will be a challenge to him. Which ever one of you averts his eyes first is the loser. It is best not to stare at your dog, since if you blink, he will think he is establishing more control.

Sleeping in Your Bed

It's not ideal for your dog to sleep with you in your bed. In his natural world, the top dog gets the best sleeping place. If you do want to let him sleep with you, invite him up and do not let him push you around as he settles in. It is best for the alpha dog training if he sleeps at the foot of the bed and not close to your pillows.

Human Emotions and Your Puppy

When you and your family are around your puppy, avoid showing emotions like nervousness, anxiety or fear. He will sense those emotions and see you as a weak leader. Think calm but big, and be consistent, assertive and calm with your puppy. Dogs can read human emotions quite easily, and you need to project your leadership whether it is spoken or not.

Caveats

You do not have to become Hitler in front of your dog. The alpha dog emotions will become more natural. You can modify the behaviour above if you feel that your place as alpha dog is fully established. Being the lead dog doesn't mean that you can't spend time snuggling with your dog. For many of us, this is why we got a dog in the first place. Just be sure that he doesn't think he is the boss.

Leash Training

Dogs must be taught to walk calmly on a lead. They don't instinctively know that they are not supposed to run ahead of you and play.

Teaching your puppy manners on the lead is a challenge, since they naturally move faster than we do. Your puppy is also probably excited about being outdoors.

Leads constrain the natural movement and behaviour of a dog. Some dogs want to be forever running, and others want to sniff everything you walk past. If you don't want your dog to pull when he is on a lead, you must never let him pull you. If you are not consistent about this, your dog will keep pulling you on walks.

Teach Your Cockapoo pup to Walk Calmly on a Lead

Dogs at dog shows and in TV ads prance beside their handlers, attentive to their desires. Dogs don't do that naturally. They had to be extensively trained in heeling. This means constant attention from you, and your puppy. Even dogs that heel are usually allowed to walk more normally on the lead when they are at home.

There are various useful methods for teaching dogs to walk on a lead without pulling. Until your puppy learns not to pull, every walk is a training session. Especially for puppies, these sessions should be short, fun and frequent.

Walking doesn't have to be the only exercise your puppy gets. He will pay more attention on a lead if you play with him first, toss a ball, and get him tired. This means he won't have as much excess energy when you take him for walks, and he will be easier to teach.

Walking without pulling can be done more easily with treats that are even tastier than the ones he probably always gets at home, just for snacks. Soft treats work well. Make sure that the treats you use are small in size, to keep your dog's mind on the training being done. Small treats also help to avoid your dog becoming overweight - train-ing can mean a lot of treats! Remember - if a lot of training and treats have taken place during the day, reduce their evening meal to ensure they don't get too many calories a day.

Walk at a steady, quick pace. If your puppy tends to run, he won't be able to stop and sniff everything you go past. You are actually more interesting to your dog when you are moving quickly, too.

Control Begins Before the Walking

If your puppy is going to pay attention to you and the lead while he walks, he must first pay attention before the walk begins. If he is very excited to go on a walk, focus on calming him first. Walk to your door and pick up his lead. If your dog begins dancing and barking, stand still until he calms down.After he is done prancing, and is standing still, reach down slowly and attach the lead to his collar. If he starts dancing and jumping, take the lead off and wait until he is quiet and calm. Repeat this until your dog will wait calmly for you to attach his lead. This seems tedious when you first start doing it, but it will certainly pay off.

On the Lead

As long as you have already trained your dog to sit and to come, even when there are distractions, you can train him to walk on the lead. Walk in whatever direction you select. If the dog reaches the end of his lead and pulls, stop dead and wait until he stops pulling. Bring him back to you at this point and have him sit. After he sits, praise him. Then resume your walking.

Whenever your puppy pulls, repeat the actions above. If he stays next to you while you walk, reward him. This will help him to learn that if he stays with you, he gets praise, and if he runs ahead, he must stop. If your puppy is enticed by a smell or wishes to eliminate, make him stop and come back to you. In this case, then allow him to eliminate or sniff the curious object. That is his reward. Follow him to the area of interest so that he doesn't pull again and disrupt the training process.

Be sure to reward your dog when he walks with slack in the lead, so he will continue learning to walk without pulling you along.

Play and socialising

Now that we've covered the behaviour and obedience sections, it's time for the real fun! Play should be an integral part of spending quality time with your Cockapoo. However, it shouldn't be confined to just human play – dogs need canine company too! This chapter has some important information about socialising your Cocka and getting him used to other dogs.

Fun Games for Dogs

Your puppy will be a better citizen if you take the time, especially when he is young, to play games with him.

Games help in keeping your dog busy, channelling his energy into activities that are constructive, rather than activities that destroy property. Playing with your dog will deepen your relationship with him and aid in establishing you as the pack leader.

Simple Rules for Dog Play

Once you establish these rules, enforce them on a consistent basis.

*   Keep your games short, rewarding and interesting. Don't keep the game going after your dog has become bored. Leave him wanting more, so his head is always "in the game".
*
*   Take breaks when you are playing. Your dog needs time to refocus his attention on you. Frequent breaks are also helpful in keeping your dog from becoming over-excited, since he may lose control of his "play" skills and go into "fight" mode.
*
*   Play a variety of games with your dog, not just throwing a ball and having him get it and bring it back to you. That is a wonderful game for dogs, but they need variety, just as you do.

Playing with a Water Hose

You can use the hose to instigate a fun game of chase with your dog. Set your nozzle so that it will shoot a jet of water. Then move it around as you spray, giving your dog something to chase. He will especially enjoy this activity on hot summer days, since he does not have sweat glands in his skin. You can give your dog a bath using the hose game too, which makes it a fun activity instead of a chore. Bathtubs often stress dogs out, and many dogs do not enjoy taking a bath. However, if your dog loves to chase water, and doesn't mind getting wet while he plays, it's a great multi-tasking tool.

Be sure you don't spray the jet of water right at your dog's face. Stop now and then and run through some of your beginner obedience training exercises, and then go back to fun. Do not let your dog jump on you during the water hose game, and don't let him try to attack the hose. If he does, stop the game and enforce your gaming rules.

Not all dogs enjoy water, so this game should not be in your itinerary if your dog is not fond of chasing water or getting wet.

Play Ball

There are many games you can play with a ball that your Cockapoo will probably love. Different types of ball games will have him more or less enthusiastic, so pick his favourite games to play most often.

Playing catch is a simple ball game that many dogs love. Toss a small ball to your puppy so that it can be easily caught by mouth. Be sure you choose a ball that is small enough that it fits in his mouth,but not so small that it could be accidentally swallowed.

Once your dog understands "Catch", you can make tosses that are a bit more difficult. It can also be played with a Frisbee, if you have a large enough area for play. If your puppy really loves playing catch with a Frisbee, you might train him to be a disc dog.

"Fetch" is a game that many dogs truly enjoy. It is not as easily taught as some other games, so take it slow at first. Make sure that your dog understands "Come" and "Drop" before you teach him to play fetch games.

Begin by giving your puppy a toy. After he holds it in his mouth, move several steps away and call him. Encourage him if he steps toward you and praise him when he comes all the way to you. After he is in front of you, tell him to "Drop" the toy and give him praise or treats when he gives you the toy.

Once your dog has comfortably learned the basics, throw a fetch toy just a short distance away. If your puppy ignores it, find a more interesting toy to use – perhaps one that squeaks.

If your dog gets the toy and brings it to you, that is cause for big celebration and much praise. However, when learning, dogs will often run to the toy, and not bring it back. He might even grab the toy and take it somewhere else to play.

Be very patient with your puppy at this stage of game training. Every time your dog brings the toy towards you, make a big fuss over him and praise him. If he leaves the toy and comes back with nothing, offer him the toy again. After he has it in his mouth, back up a few steps and call to him, with a lot of enthusiasm in your voice. Praise him a lot if he comes toward you with the toy.

If your dog decides to run off with his toy or dares you to catch him if you can, you may need a tastier treat to help him learn. Don't chase your dog, since that rewards him for running away, which is definitely something you don't want to do.

Not every dog enjoys playing fetch. If your dog doesn't think it's a fun game, choose another.

Soccer or football is a fun game to play with your dog. The idea is kicking the ball away from your dog, and getting him to chase it. Once he gets to the ball, allow him to play with it before you kick it again.

You need a larger ball for soccer, and one that is difficult to puncture. Rubber balls work well. The ball should be large enough that your puppy cannot hold it in his mouth. This will make it easier for you to kick away from him, too.

Your dog might prefer chasing balls that squeak, so get him one if that pleases him in the game play. You can even dab a little peanut butter on the ball so that he will want it even more.

Socialising with other dogs

Socialising teaches your Cockapoo to be a part of a larger society. Socialising puppies means aiding them in becoming comfortable as pets within our human society. Our society includes many people, noises, smells, sights – and other dogs.

Most puppies will eventually become accustomed to the things encountered in their new environment, but this is only true until a certain age is reached. Once your dog reaches that age, he will be more suspicious of new things. This is Mother Nature at work. She allows a younger puppy to become more comfortable with new things that are a part of his puppy life, so that he won't spend his whole life being frightened of non-scary things.

The suspicion developed by dogs as they age ensures that they react with healthy caution to new environmental stimuli that may be dangerous.

When Should You Socialise Your Puppy?

Your puppy will most readily accept new experiences between the ages of three and 12 weeks. After 12 weeks of age, they will become more cautious of new things. After 18 weeks, your opportunity to socialise your puppy easily will end. Every week after that makes it harder for you to encourage your puppy to accept new things.
If your puppy is well socialised, he will generally develop into a more relaxed, safer and enjoyable pet to have around. This is due to his comfort in many situations. He will be less likely to be aggressive or fearful in reaction to new situations. Relaxed dogs react in a more predictable way to everything, including vets, cats, hoovers, crowds and other new things. If your puppy is properly socialised, he will also have a peaceful, more relaxed and happier life than dogs whose environment stresses them out.

Socialisation can be done a little bit or a lot. The more new experiences he is exposed to as a young puppy, the better his chances will be of becoming a dog that is comfortable in many different situations.

How to Socialise Your Cockapoo

Socialising your dog should be an important project for you and your puppy. Your puppy will need to be exposed to all types of animals, people, sounds, experiences and places in which you want him to be comfortable, as he grows older.

Depending on where you live, this may include school playgrounds full of noisy, lively children, loud lorries, cats, crowds, crying babies or other animals. You won't be able to expose your puppy to literally everything he might see later in life, but the more he sees when he is young, the more likely he will be to be reassured in new situations. When you socialise your puppy, don't place him in situations that overwhelm him. He should get more – not less – comfortable when exposed to the same situation again. If meeting a room full of other puppies is too much for him right now, then have just one person and their puppy come over first, and work from there.

Always watch how your puppy reacts to new situations. Be ready to lessen the stimuli if your dog becomes frightened. After every experience with socialisation, praise your dog and give him a special treat or some special time with you.

Puppy Classes

Socialising a puppy is helped by attending "nursery or kindergarten" classes for puppies. These are specifically designed for training your puppy in socialisation. Playing off-lead and pretend fighting allow puppies to meet others and play. They will learn to be gentle when they are mouthing or biting and they will become accustomed to being handled by more people. Some classes use CDs of sounds, along with props, to expose puppies to strange sounds and sights. These classes also impart a few basic obedience skills, so that makes them doubly helpful.

Tips and tools for training your Cockapoo

Now that we've covered the basics, this section will go through some final tips and tricks to remember when training your Cocka. Following these guidelines will help you to train your Cocka into a well behaved little dog.

1. Start with simple commands and increase the difficulty gradually.

You will want to proceed step-by-step so that you're giving your puppy plenty of practice time to get the commands right. Start with the easier commands, and do them in familiar places without lots of distractions. After your dog is more predictable in his responses, and doing what you want him to do, then add distractions and distance.

You will stand close to your dog when you are first training a new command. After he understands it and responds properly, take a step back, and then another, until he will perform the command without your being right next to him.

Allow your dog to learn one command well before you begin another. If he doesn't perform well, remove a distraction and try the command again. Always be willing to slow down and go back to the last point at which he was performing the command response properly.

2. Be consistent in your commands

Always use the same command word for each command you are teaching your dog. If you say "Come" sometimes and "Come here" at other times, it is confusing for your dog.

3. Treats make good rewards

There are many training methods you can use, but using edible treats will allow you to lure your dog and reward him when he responds properly. If your puppy is not interested in food, give him lots of verbal praise and perhaps one of his favourite toys. Scratching behind his ears or in another favourite spot is also a good reward.

4. Do not repeat your commands

You may do this without thinking, but it doesn't help your dog. In fact, it teaches him that he doesn't have to come the first time he is called.

5. Be patient

Yelling or jerking your dog's lead will not teach him how to come or to sit. Instead, it will teach him that you are unpredictable and loud, and that training is not a fun thing. When you feel yourself growing impatient, return to to something he does easily and then end the training session. Your dog will respect and obey you if you are calm, consistent and fair.

6. Phase out your rewards

Your dog may be more motivated when you reward him in ways he cannot predict. Once your dog knows the commands, only use treats if he does very well on his response. Vary the frequency, amount and type of reward and add praise and tummy rubs as you give fewer food treats. You won't always have treats with you when you need him to respond to your commands.

7. Keep training sessions short

Training is more effective when it is fun for your dog. Stop before you or your dog are bored. Keep sessions shorter rather than longer, and don't be a bossy person to your dog. Five to ten minutes is fine for a first training session, and mini trainings can be done any time of the day.

8. Add new people and new places

Give your dog his commands in different settings, once he has the idea of what you want. In this way, he will also respond properly to family members or friends who might be dog sitting for you sometime in the future.

9. Allow your dog to earn his treats

After your dog knows some commands, ask him to obey one before giving him a toy or a treat, or a scratch behind the ears. If he doesn't respond to your command, do not give him what he wants just yet. Wait a minute and try again. Then reward him when he obeys you.

10. Practice never ends

Just because your dog learns to "come" does not mean that he will remember it forever. He can lose his skills if you don't practice them regularly.

Mastering the skills of basic obedience training is important for you and your dog. They make the relationship more harmonious and will keep your puppy and you safe if there are emergencies in the future. Training a dog takes a lot of patient work.

Any dog is capable of learning the basic commands. If you have a bad day of training, don't be frustrated. Just try again when you are both in a better frame of mind. If you need help, seek out a professional trainer.

You are responsible for fully socialising and training your dog. Understand the amount of time it will take before you adopt a puppy or dog, so that he will be well trained and happy with you.

Remember, having a dog should be fun. Don't take everything too seriously, and be sure that you and your dog have good times when you are training him. This will make him more receptive in future training sessions.

Things to Remember during Training

When you are first training, select an area that is not full of distractions for your Cockapoo. Once the commands are mastered, you can move to areas with more distractions and feel confident that he will still respond to your commands. If you have two dogs, remember you can only train one at a time – with two dogs you won't have their total concentration, they will distract each other. Group training can come later once your dogs have learned the basics.

Use verbal praise and petting as rewards. Food treats are great, and they will entice your dog to perform properly. However, you may find yourself in situations where no treats are available, and he needs to respond to you properly without expecting food every time. Toys can also be given as a reward, especially if they are his favourite toys, but remember once again that in an emergency, you may not have toys with you to use to lure your dog.

Short leads are great for walking, but longer leads or long lines will work better for any training where you are placing distance between you and your dog. Make sure you are confident that he will come when called and follow other verbal commands before you work with him without a long line attached. It can be left on the ground, only to be used if your dog decides that a nice run in the opposite direction sounds like fun.

Your training sessions should always end with a positive response from your dog. If he is having trouble learning a new command, and you've been working with him for a little while, go back to a command he knows, and reward him for executing that response correctly. This way, he'll look forward to his next training session.

Canine Good Citizen Classes

Most national Kennel Club's run Good Citizen Classes and you should contact them to find out where the classes are being run in your area. In the US, The American Kennel Club (AKC) offers a program that rewards dogs who become good canine citizens. It began in 1989, and it rewards your dog if he has good manners, both at home and out in the city or community.

There are two parts to the Canine Good Citizen classes. They both stress that you need to be a responsible pet owner and that your dog should be a pleasure for others to be around. Any dog that passes the 10-step test for Canine Good Citizenship is eligible for a certificate issued by the AKC. In the UK, The Kennel Club runs a Good Citizen Class and these classes were started in 1982 and operate along similar lines to the US Classes.

The Canine Good Citizen Program Is a Good Foundation

The Canine Good Citizen program is a good first step for training your Cockapoo. It will lay a proper foundation for any other Kennel Club activities that you might like to participate in, for example obedience, performance, agility and tracking. As you teach your dog CGC skills, you will be happy to discover the joys and benefits of successfully training your puppy.

Training enhances the bond that exists between you and your puppy. If your dog has a solid education in obedience, he will respond better to you and will be a more pleasant dog with which to live. In addition, your puppy will enjoy your company even more after training, since it strengthens the bond you have with your dog.

Often, Canine Good Citizen training will give you and your dog sessions that are stimulating intellectually, and this will help your dog in developing a higher quality of life. CGC is often just the beginning of a long life of successful training, in whatever types of events you think might be enjoyable for both of you.

The Popularity of a Kennel Club Canine Good Citizen Program

This program is one of the Kennel Clubs' training areas of rapid growth. The entry-level program gives you and your dog a good foundation for future training. Many countries have developed programmes. Animal control and police agencies use this program when they deal with dog issues in communities. Some groups that train therapy dogs also use CGC as a screening tool. In addition, some groups use the CGC program to teach children beginner dog training.

Some speciality breed clubs, for single breeds only, give the Canine Good Citizen award programme at their yearly national dog shows. Members of clubs for dogs of all breeds realise that CGC is a popular event that lets everyone who competes become a winner. Vets appreciate dogs that are well trained, and there are more than a few CGC programmes in veterinary hospitals.

Even though the CGC programmes have not been in existence for a long time, they have had a positive impact in many communities. It can help you to assure yourself that your beloved dog will always be a well-respected and welcomed member of your community.

Companion dog Training

Companion dog training is an excellent way to teach your dog to be responsive to you, even in situations when emergencies arise. Working with your dog in companion dog training allows him to become better socialised, which means that he can retain knowledge more easily. As your puppy matures, he will be less likely to bite, and will be calmer around other dogs and other people.

Training in groups gives you a few advantages, even if training at home has been successful. If you and your dog are in a situation that has many distractions, you will want to know that you can still count on your dog to obey your commands without hesitation.

Certification Requirements

There are certain requirements of Companion Dog Program Dogs and their owners. They have adopted these requirements since you and your dog may encounter a wide variety of ordinary situations while meeting other dogs and owners in public settings. Trained CDP teams can work in the park system, and as such, they must behave as calm and professional teams.

Companion dogs must be able to respond calmly and instantly obey your commands, even in stressful circumstances.

CDP teams may represent the areas in which they were trained. When you and your dog pass this programme, you can set a good example for other dogs and their owners.

Companion Dog Testing

Companion Dogs must pass an annual test with control and confidence. The actual test is extended from the Canine Good Citizen Program testing. It will involve you, your dog and an evaluator who has been properly trained and certified.

Your dog must be able to:

1. Walk easily on even a loose lead

This will demonstrate that you are in control of your dog. You may allow your dog to walk on either side of you, whichever you prefer. You must include an about turn, a right turn and a left turn, with one or more stops between them. Your dog will need to calmly stop at the end of this exercise, too. Your dog does not have to sit whenever you stop.

2. Accept friendly strangers

This part of the CDT test will demonstrate that your dog will allow someone he does not know to approach him in a friendly way, while the stranger speaks to you. You and the evaluator, who plays the part of the stranger, will shake hands and talk for a few minutes. Your dog must not show shyness or resentment, and cannot break his position or try to walk up and meet the stranger.

3. Have attractive grooming and appearance

This will demonstrate that your dog will allow himself to be groomed and examined, such as might be carried out by a dog groomer or vet. Your dog should allow a friend to examine and groom him. This also will demonstrate your concern, responsibility and caring for your dog. The evaluator will inspect your dog, comb or brush him and examine both front feet and his ears.

4. Sit politely while being petted

This test will show that your dog will allow a person he does not know to touch him in a friendly way while he is out with you. Your dog will

91

sit at your side, and the evaluator will pet your dog on his body and head. He will then circle you and your dog. Your dog cannot show resentment or shyness.

5. Walk through a crowd

In this test, your dog must move politely among pedestrians, and remain under control when you are out in public places. You and your dog will walk around close to three or more people. It is acceptable for your dog to show interest in a stranger, as long as he is not over-exuberant or excessively shy. You may speak to your dog, to praise and encourage him. He should not be pulling on his lead.

6. Obey sit, down and stay

This test will demonstrate that your dog has been trained and will respond to your commands. You may use more than a few seconds to help your dog obey, and you may even use more than one command. In the "stay" phase, you will tell your dog to stay, and walk forward for 20 feet. Your dog may change positions, but must remain where he is.

7. Come when you call

Your dog should always come to you when you call him. In this test, you will walk 10 feet away from your dog, then face him and call him. You are allowed to add body language if you need it, and encouragement. You may ask your dog to wait or stay, or you can walk from him without verbal cues. The evaluator will pet your dog a bit, to provide a mild distraction.

8. Show little reaction to other dogs

This part of the test will demonstrate that your dog is polite with other dogs. You and another handler will walk toward each other, shake hands and speak, then continue on. Your dog should not have anything more than casual interest in the other dog.

9. Show minimal reaction to distraction

Your dog should be confident even when faced with common situations that may be distracting, like someone running by or dropping something. He may show a natural curiosity or interest, but he should not bark, show aggressiveness, attempt to run away, or panic.

10. Interact with animals in a park setting

Your dog should remain under control without reacting adversely to any other animals you may encounter in parks. Horses, dogs or other animals may be used to test your dog. The rider of the horse or handler of the other animal will stop and chat with you, then continue on their way. A whole group of dogs and handlers or horses and riders will mill about, close to your dog. Your dog should only show a casual interest.

11. Be calm when separated from you and unsupervised

Your dog should keep his good manners and training when you leave him alone. The evaluator may ask if you would like him to watch your dog, and he will hold your dog's leash. Your dog will be with the evaluator for three minutes. He doesn't have to stay in the same position, but he cannot pace, whine, bark or howl, or display any emotions other than mild nervousness or agitation.

12. React calmly to emergency vehicles

Your dog should remain fully under control even when close to emergency vehicles. He should remain in position while vehicles go by quickly, with sirens and lights on. The emergency vehicle will block the trail on which you and your dog are walking. An actor playing a "victim" will be attended to on the ground. You and your dog will walk by and you will ask if there is anything you can do to help. Your dog should remain under control and cannot shy away from the unusual sights and sounds.

Conclusion

Congratulations! In this book, you've managed to learn about some important aspects of welcoming a new Cockapoo into your home. You should also have a good idea about the best ways to make your dog a good companion and a welcome family member. By now, you should be familiar with the wide spectrum of behaviours you can expect from your canine companion.

Take the time to enjoy hours spent training your Cockapoo – a few minutes at a time, since his attention span is not very long. After you have bonded with your dog, you will be confident to take him out whenever you want. Don't let bad behaviour go unchallenged, or it will become a lasting habit. Instead, use the techniques in this book to train out bad behaviour and replace it with obedient responses.
If you attend a specific training club in your area, and you feel that it has benefited you and your dog, recommend the club when you speak to new dog owners. This will help to get them started off on the right paw, too.

We hope you enjoy becoming a Cockapoo owner and all the joy and fun it brings! Don't hesitate to get in touch with your local vet if you have any questions – they are always happy to help.

The writer of this book, Dr. Gordon Roberts, is a veterinarian and owns a total of eight animal hospitals around the UK. He believes that the key to a healthy, happy pet is preventative care, which is only possible when pet owners take the initiative to educate themselves about their animals. As a result, Gordon has written dozens of useful reports on pet care in order to share his years of experience with discerning pet owners. As a thank you for purchasing this book, you can browse and download his specialist reports completely free of charge! You'll learn all sorts of useful information about how to spot possible health conditions early on, and how to make preventative care for your pet a priority, helping you save time and money on visits to the vet later on. To view and download these bonus reports, simply visit Gordon's website at: http://drgordonroberts.com/freereportsdownload/.

Best wishes,
Gordon

Printed in Great Britain
by Amazon